AF612360

Antonio "Ike" DeVargas

Norteño Warrior

Antonio "Ike" DeVargas
Norteño Warrior

The Politics of Land, Power, and Justice
in Northern New Mexico

Kay Matthews

Antonio "Ike" DeVargas — Norteño Warrior: The Politics of Land, Power, and Justice in Northern New Mexico. Copyright 2026 by Kay Matthews.

All rights reserved, including those to reproduce this book, or parts thereof, in any form, without permission, other than in the case of brief quotations embodied in critical articles and reviews. For permission requests, write to the publisher, Attention Permissions Coordinator at Nighthawk Press, PO Box 1222, Taos NM 87571. nighthawkpress.com

First edition, 2026

ISBN: 979-8-9888976-3-7

Library of Congress Control Number: 2026906856

Printed in the United States

Photographs are from the La Jicarita Archive and the DeVargas Estate, unless otherwise attributed. Thanks to Elisa DeVargas for their use.

Cover photo by Eric Shultz

Design by Kelly Pasholk, Wink Visual Arts LLC

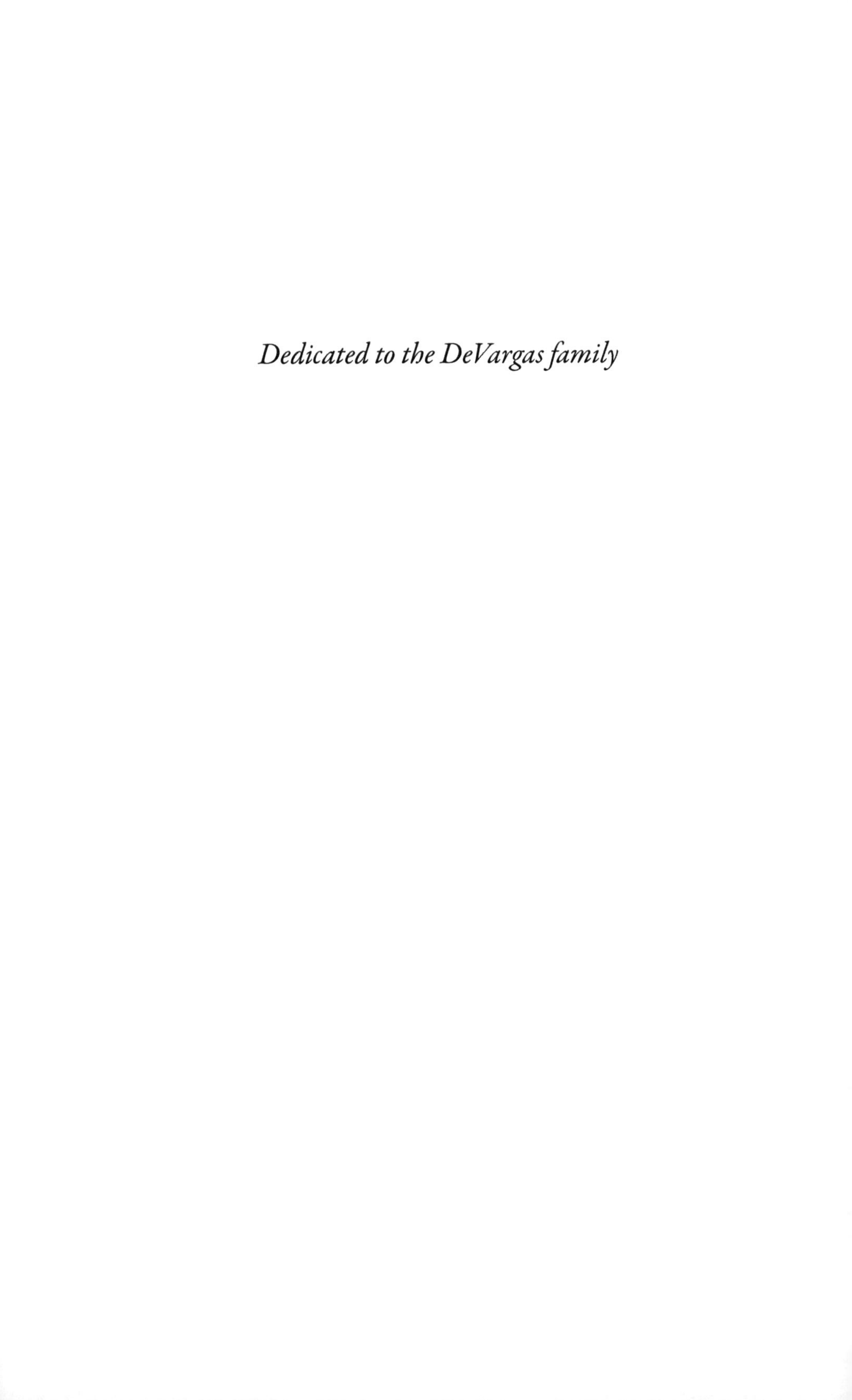

Dedicated to the DeVargas family

Table of Contents

Foreword

Antonio "Ike" DeVargas was my father's best friend and *camarada* (comrade) for nearly five decades. He was our next-door neighbor for many years, living in a small one-bedroom house we referred to as La Casa Vieja. Years later, he purchased a couple of acres of land from my grandmother on the south end of Servilleta Plaza, where he made his permanent home. Having such proximity to Ike made him larger than life and, at the same time, very human. I often found myself reading newspaper articles covering his latest effort against the US Forest Service while listening to my dad complain that he'd borrowed and hadn't returned his tools. From my first days of elementary school up through the birth of my youngest child, Ike was always around, splitting wood or skinning an elk in the garage with my dad—Luis "Loco"—and a few of the bros or sitting around the dinner table in *plática* discussing the events of the day.

In 1993, my mother Renee went into premature labor with my youngest sister. She was home alone and unable to drive, but thankfully, Ike was next door. He acted swiftly and drove her to the nearest hospital nearly an hour away. My sister was born months premature and remained in an incubator while her lungs finished developing. My parents named her Angela, the angel of our family and a miracle of modern science. Ike saved her life and forever changed the narrative of our familia. Ike's heroics showed up time and time again when my dad went missing in a snowstorm or when the sheriffs were threatening to raid the family compound. There was Ike, a former Marine with skills forged in the conflict of Vietnam, and we knew we could always count on him.

On the surface, Ike was a rank-and-file Norteño, a real meat-and-potatoes kind of guy. He owned way too many chainsaws and no fewer than four or five dogs at a time. After his last divorce, as a bachelor, dinner often consisted of whatever he could fit in a crockpot. But as I grew older and took an interest in reading, I began to understand the depth of his intelligence. I would often borrow books from him and discuss what I learned. He would set aside books that he knew I would appreciate, such as Luis Rodriguez's *Always Running: La Vida Loca, Gang Days in LA,* Rodolfo Acuña's *Occupied America,* or the music of Peter Tosh. He was also versed in the esoteric arts, a self-proclaimed Rosicrucian, and the owner of at least one dashiki. He practiced tai chi in the mornings and probably had a crystal ball lying around. I remember once he loaned me some books on magic divination and told me, "Don't tell your dad, he wouldn't understand." My dad viewed anything that deviated from Catholicism with disapproval and often warned me not to let some of the stuff Ike believed in "burn my mind."

Ike's strength was in his connection to the land and the people. If you wanted to know where to hunt or gather osha, Ike was a wealth of knowledge. He was well-liked and respected in the community among elders and children alike. I think that, in another life, he could have been a scholar whose work was published in dissertations within the halls of academia. But because he was created from the genetic material of the surrounding mountains, he became a genuine leader elevated by his own people. As Richard Rosenstock, Ike's longtime friend and attorney, once stated, "There are many activists around but very few who are leaders. Ike DeVargas was a leader. He did not fear the consequences, and they are always there, of being out front on issues of social and economic justice.

Ike was part of a generation of men who were sent off to fight for a colonial power, only to come home to the realization that they, too, were colonized by the very same forces. Ike shared with me that the death of his grandfather broke him in a way that propelled him out into the world and straight into the US Marines. He shared stories of living in Watts through the riots of 1965, of being trained in guerrilla tactics on remote Pacific islands, and of the constant threat of death that came with challenging the status quo in Rio Arriba County. He often commented that he went to Vietnam to fight a dictatorship, only to find another dictatorship at home when he returned. He was referring to the political machine of Emilio Naranjo.

Chairman Huey P. Newton of the Oakland chapter of the Black Panther Party for Self-Defense once famously defined politics as "the ability to define a phenomenon and cause it to act in a desired manner." When the Chicano Movement emerged in northern New Mexico, it drew from the experience of an older land grant movement that had been shaped over a century of struggle. The land grant movement, in turn, stemmed from a rich history of resistance established by regional revolts and uprisings in the 17th and 18th centuries, as well as insurgent groups such as the La Mano Negra and the Gorras Blancas. In the 1970s, *Chicanismo* had awakened within a national cultural consciousness and found purpose in opposing the ongoing war in Vietnam, confronting police violence in the barrio, and advocating for labor rights and improved community infrastructure. The Tierra Amarilla Court House raid of 1967 prompted many young Chicanos to embrace northern New Mexico and elevate the movement to recognize land grants as a matter of international treaty. La Raza Unida Party became a regional platform for organizing efforts in land and water tenure, rural healthcare, legal aid, and running candidates for state and local governance positions. It was disruptive to the prevailing social order of the time and garnered both negative and positive attention. My family experienced all of this on a very personal level, the impacts of which are still felt to this day.

I was born in 1977 when the fires of the Chicano Movement were raging and came of age when they burned down to *brazas* (embers). When I was a boy, the red and black symbol of the Thunderbird was still emblazoned on flags and license plates throughout The Norte, but much of the movement's energy had shifted towards the Democratic Party or academic institutions. On the streets of Española, the thump of the boombox and the illuminated signs of chain restaurants began to take prominence. I became a teenager watching gambling and opiate addiction carve into the landscape and add to the existing pressure of poverty and rural isolation. In 2001, after the 9/11 attacks, things shifted further in our corner of the world. The Department of Homeland Security and the Patriot Act fine-tuned the export of imperial violence abroad, a new domestic surveillance state was empowered and a new generation of Norteños was sent off to fight in a foreign land.

Through all of this, I relied on Ike to help me navigate how we had arrived in this place and where we were going from there. Watching the evening news with him was one of my favorite pastimes. He would take in the news in its entirety and then explain the bigger picture of what it all meant, nervously flicking his cigarette. Although some of his analyses could be considered opinion, they offered up insight for my evolving worldview. Through waves of sociopolitical change, I could count on Ike to provide enough perspective to prompt me to read further and develop my own opinion. As if by magic, Ike foretold many of the societal ills we are struggling with today under the current administration. Through it all, he kept his view laser focused at the local level. He once playfully prodded his nephew Adam's idealism with the inquiry, "How are you going to fight the global elite when we can't even get a corrupt sheriff out of office?"

The life of an activist can be hard, however, and the unfortunate reality is that the immediate family often carries the weight. With so much focus on the activism, partners and kids can often fade into the background and play second fiddle to "the cause." Oftentimes, activists find themselves fighting for resources—basic healthcare, mental health, substance abuse—that are denied to their own families because of systemic neglect. I lived through some very scary times when bounties were placed on my dad's and Ike's heads, and we would have to hide my dad in the trunk of the car for a simple trip into town. My mother was always worried she would have to bail them out of jail and would often joke that they weren't allowed to hang out together because they caused too much trouble.

In writing this introduction, I want to ensure that Ike's family is recognized for their efforts in supporting his work. They shared him with the world, but in his passing, the grief and loss are theirs to hold. The Norte lost a hero and an icon, but his family lost a father, a grandfather, an uncle, a brother, and a primo. Men like Ike can cast a long shadow that can be difficult to live under, yet the DeVargas clan shines as a genetic saga of everything that makes northern New Mexico beautiful and unique. As a result of the *compadrazco* between the Peña and DeVargas families, I have borne witness to a lifetime of tragedy and triumph, success and failure, joy and pain. Ike was a man full of life's contradictions. He fought for basic healthcare for the most remote regions of northern New Mexico, yet his own daughter was denied healthcare that resulted in her tragic death. He was a direct descendant of Don Diego DeVargas, Spanish governor during the Reconquest of New Mexico, yet he fought on the right side of history against corrupt Rio Arriba County officials, direct descendants of Domingo Naranjo, a primary instigator of the Pueblo Revolt of 1680. This dynamic is a master lesson in the fluidity of race, class, and identity in New Mexico. Ike was humble to a fault, but defiantly self-assured, critical of US foreign policy, yet a proud American veteran. As a soldier in the 1st Reconnaissance Battalion, he featured on the cover of *Time Magazine*, was buried with high honors, and was eligible for a military flyover. His family was stunned that he never made mention of his decorations. Even in the end, it seems Ike DeVargas found balance and purpose in the unpredictable.

As an adult who has raised children of my own, I have come to appreciate the significance of Ike's work, the efforts of the Chicano Movement, and the broader movement towards liberation across the globe. I realize that, thanks to the sacrifices of those who came before me, I was blessed to have been raised free in the mountains of northern

New Mexico. I was lucky to have had teachers and mentors who were from the families that made up my community and who knew me, my parents, and the countless generations before me. They mirrored perspectives that I carry to this day and that I hope I have passed down to my own children. I am part of an interconnected web of kinship that has been nurtured across centuries and that carries stories of survival and hardship. This is the love that leaders carry for their people and inspires them to struggle.

Many men in my life made me who I am; I learned from their wisdom and their mistakes. I understood that becoming a man meant finding my own path, not simply mimicking theirs. I process the world around me with limited understanding, and I find joy in balancing theory and praxis in the place that raised me. I am flawed, and that makes me human. I am forever grateful for men like Ike, who embraced my wife and kids and gave me examples of what an honorable man can be. In the years following their passing, people will gift me stories of my father and Ike: hunting trips, random encounters in the forest, or observations of their shenanigans within the community. I have been in sacred spaces where their names are called out in candlelit oratorios, because the community remembers, and I do too. I often think of their sayings:

"Come on, mijo, that's popcorn!"

"The world is your oyster, cabron!"

"You'd better learn because I'm not always going to be around."

. . . . . .

A few months before Ike's death, I stopped by to visit with him. He had been recovering from a cardiac event and a recent bout of COVID, and my wife had sent him and his grandson, Andres, soup and groceries. He shared a lucid dream that he had a few nights before and expressed how significant the vision was, as he had rarely dreamed since his time in Vietnam. In the dream, he conveyed that he was in a vulnerable state and that my father came to rescue him, hiding him in a cavern deep inside a mountain while he went to find help. He noted the curiosity that my father was moving about rapidly, like a movie that was sped up, ridiculous to the point where it made him laugh. Upon hearing of Ike's death, I understood that his refuge was in the metaphorical chambers of his own heart and possibly an omen of the cardiac arrest that was to come.

When Ike passed, it was a busy time leading up to Angela's wedding. I was on my way to Albuquerque to deliver a large wooden cross for her wedding ceremony. The first call came in on my cellphone, then another, and then my phone began to "blow up" with incoming calls and text messages. I stopped and took the news in, accepting it as fact. I called Richard, and then I called Kay. I looked to the north and observed a large raincloud rising curiously like a column high above the sky. I immediately called my spiritual brother from Cochiti Pueblo, and he explained that the cloud people had come to welcome Ike home. Ike passed away at his cousin Reggie's home in Llanito de La Madera, across the street from where he grew up with his grandparents, in a final act of service, providing care and comfort to a loved one in need. At that moment, we were all united in our disbelief at imagining a world without him. Angela was married a few days later, and she held a memorial spot for him at her wedding, one that he'd promised to attend and one I believe he kept even in death. Ike was buried in his signature flannel and jeans—the humble uniform of a *cerreño* (mountain man) from northern New Mexico—not a suit and tie that would have made him look uncomfortably out of place.

As a final act of resistance, Ike and I collaborated on stopping the installation of the statue of Juan de Onate at the Rio Arriba County Complex in 2023. Kay tells this story in detail in the book: It was a master class on civic engagement and navigating the systems of power at the state and local level, and I will forever be grateful for the experience. I come from a place of deep gratitude to Kay for taking on this task to document Ike's lifelong effort to champion justice in a region of the world that has been denied due process for generations. Northern New Mexico is a curious place where unexpected things happen, where a strong memory of rebellion and resistance remains, and in that understanding, hope exists. One day, our people will achieve our liberation, and we will have the memory of Ike's strength and struggle as our north star.

Asi sea.

Hermano Luis Peña
Española, New Mexico
Occupied Aztlán

Introduction

Environmental Outlaw

The winter snows, not lawsuits, temporarily quieted the chainsaws in the Vallecitos Valley of northern New Mexico. As spring approached, however, the Indo-Hispano people who traditionally made their living through small-scale logging and ranching on public lands, anticipated renewed legal efforts by environmental groups to shut down these land-based activities. Norteños saw the lawsuits as an assault on their livelihood, their traditions, their culture. The environmental groups, led by the Santa Fe-based Forest Guardians, in their zeal to protect biodiversity and threatened species, failed to acknowledge that the land-based people of northern New Mexico were part of the ecosystem.

In a 1997 visit to New Mexico Interior Secretary Bruce Babbitt remarked that the Southwest had seen more controversy and strife than other areas of the country where collaborative efforts between government, environmentalists, and local forest users had been successful. In fact, the New Mexico battles between environmental groups like Forest Guardians and norteños engendered internecine fights within the environmental community, extending beyond the boundaries of the Southwest.

Environmental justice issues are not new to the movement. Witness the fracture of Greenpeace over Native rights issues or the departure of Dave Foreman from Earth First! because the group was "leaning too far left." However, the conflict in New Mexico added new a dimension to the issue: Here, in the "inhabited wilderness" of former Spanish and Mexican land grants that were supposed to be protected by the 1848 Treaty of Guadalupe Hidalgo, norteños were the vanguard of *la lucha*, the struggle to keep people connected to land and community, an invaluable environmental strategy against the encroachment of corporate globalization.

The Vallecitos Valley, home to the small logging outfit La Companía de Ocho, was at the epicenter of the controversy: La Companía's right to log the La Manga timber sale was blocked for three years by various lawsuits filed by Forest Guardians. Antonio "Ike" DeVargas, a founding member of La Companía de Ocho and long-time norteño activist since the La Raza Unida Party days of the 1970s, consistently pointed out the failure of environmental groups to differentiate between sustainable, community-based logging, which can promote the health of second-growth forests by thinning overcrowded stands (only one percent of trees 24 inches in diameter would be cut in the La Manga sale), and the corporate rape of northern New Mexico forests that exploited both the resources and the people. The Vallecitos Valley is also part of a federally mandated Federal Sustained Yield Unit, set aside in the 1940s to directly benefit impoverished rural communities. For years the US Forest Service set timber quotas too high for competitive bids from small operators, and Duke City Lumber, a multi-national logging corporation, enjoyed a virtual monopoly in the valley.

DeVargas and other activists fought to have Duke City kicked out of the Sustained Yield Unit and to reduce the huge numbers of board feet being cut. Finally, in 1994, La Companía filed suit against the Forest Service for failing to meet the requirements of the Sustained Yield Act and for racial discrimination, and in 1996 was awarded seventy percent of the La Manga sale. But Forest Guardians had already filed suit against the timber sale, and the battle lines were drawn. Sam Hitt, president of Forest Guardians, called DeVargas an "environmental outlaw" and promoter of "Green Hate," while DeVargas and other activists twice hung Hitt in effigy.

……

Who was this so-called "environmental outlaw"? I first encountered DeVargas, who I will refer to as Ike ("Ike" comes from his middle name, Isaac, and is pronounced Ikey), in Danny Lyon's film "Little Boy," made in 1977 and named for the atomic bomb made in New Mexico and dropped on Hiroshima. The film is about much more than the bomb, however, and one of the "beneath the sunbelt" things it looks at is New Mexico's La Raza Unida Party. A founding member of the Party, Ike is interviewed in a house in the tiny village of Servilleta Plaza where he's seen combing the hair of his young son, Antonio, while he talks about taking on police violence and stolen land grants in Rio Arriba County.

Danny Lyon video "Little Boy"

Lyon's camera zooms in on Ike's head full of dark curls and light-colored eyes—the film is black and white—to profile this hard-edged Chicano activist. He's just been arrested and released for pistol-whipping an off-duty cop at the Chamisa Inn in Española, a cop who had been harassing La Raza Unida Party members trying to overthrow the corrupt county patron, Emilio Naranjo. Lyon asks Ike if he thinks he'll survive prison if he gets convicted. "No, they'll kill me if I end up there."

Ike and his son Antonio

The first time I met Ike in person was in the early 1990s, in the same house in Servilleta Plaza (he was staying there waiting for his trailer to be hooked up to utilities) when I went to interview him for a book I planned to write on forest politics. A lot had happened to him in those intervening years; his curly black hair was completely white, his blue eyes surrounded by wrinkles, but he was just as intense as he was back in the seventies. He'd survived a short stint in the state prison for beating up the cop—the charges were dropped—but he was in the thick of it again, this time battling both the US Forest Service and urban environmentalists over community access to resources. He had just organized a demonstration at environmental lawyer Grove Burnett's private ranch outside the village of Vallecitos (down the road from Servilleta Plaza), protesting a gathering of national environmental activists. He was getting ready to make the long drive to Tierra Amarilla, the county seat, to meet with Ganados del Valle, a local agricultural cooperative that was involved in a lawsuit with the Sierra Club over alleged mismanagement of a grant dispersed through the Sierra Club but intended for Ganados. "You know," he said, "logging isn't an easy job. I'd gladly give it up if there was anything else I could do. But that's what this is all about, getting the powers that be to recognize that we're always going to be here and we have to make a living. You can shut down the woods, but we still aren't leaving. We were here *before* there was timbering."

As co-editor of *La Jicarita News*, a journal of environmental politics, with my partner Mark Schiller, we engaged with Ike as both journalists and members of the norteño community. We began publishing the newspaper in 1996 as part of a watershed coalition based in the Peñasco area, advocating for water resources, particularly the acequias, or irrigation ditches that provide water to all the small communities throughout northern New Mexico. We also had our share of controversy over US Forest Service policy and community access to forest resources, and the paper quickly expanded to cover these issues across all of el norte. Ike was at the forefront of these battles, as both a legendary community organizer and a founding member of La Companía de Ocho. We went out with him to the proposed timber sales to look at the site prescriptions. We attended all the meetings involving the Forest Service, environmentalists, and community activists, both adversarial and productive. We attended all the demonstrations where Ike and his comrades vented their frustrations and hopes. We went to parties at his house in Servilleta Plaza, and he came to parties at our house in El Valle. We danced at the Chamisa Inn in Española, celebrated the school graduations of one daughter, mourned the death of another, and became lifelong friends.

This book is a profile of Ike's political life, not a biography. While I knew him as both a friend and colleague, I focus here on the evolution of his political activism. Chapter One traces the beginning of his political awakening in the jungles of Vietnam where he witnessed firsthand American imperialism against a developing nation. Once home, he recognized that the same forces were at work against the Hispano and Native American communities in northern New Mexico under the rule of a despotic Rio Arriba County official. La Raza Unida Party became the vehicle for change. Chapter Two follows La Raza's segue into Democratic progressive politics, which Ike didn't see as much of an improvement in the political machine. For his own sanity he returned to the woods to make a living and reconnect with the work that had always tied him to land and community. He eventually formed his own small logging company, La Companía de Ocho, to try to wrest control of local timbering from corporate hands. Chapter Three is the long, disappointing slog through the environmental lawsuits that plagued his company and the efforts of other norteños who wanted a vested interest in their local economies. Battling both US Forest Service mismanagement and urban environmentalists left many of these efforts, including La Companía's, futile. Chapter Four investigates national policies like "Zero Cut," no logging on public lands, that contributed to the confrontations between environmentalists and community-based foresters. Chapter Five documents the last timber sale assigned to La Companía that lingered for three years in litigation before signaling the demise of the company.

Chapter Six follows Ike's activism after a period of political burnout and a series of chronic health problems he needed to address. It leaves forest politics to focus on events that again evoked his innate commitment to social justice. He took on Rio Arriba County when he discovered that the dysfunctional solid waste company was billing people illegally—including Ike—and the county wasn't doing anything about it. In some ways it was a return to the La Raza Unida Party days of demanding accountability of a corrupt political machine. That machine went on to become embroiled in the contentious racial policies that surrounded the statue of Spanish Conquistador Juan de Oñate as it traveled from one contested site to another. Chapter Seven is the heartbreaking story of the death of his daughter Carmela due to the negligence of the Santa Fe County Adult Detention Facility. As in so many other stories, this most personally tragic event grew into a much larger demand for social justice, this time in the criminal justice system. The Final Chapter wraps up stories that hadn't previously found conclusions and ends with Ike's death in 2024.

This book is not an objective look at the politics in which he was involved. Hopefully, it will demonstrate why and how these politics evolved by focusing on his personal growth as a Chicano activist and the influence he wielded within the norteño communities struggling for economic viability and autonomy. His story is the larger story of northern New Mexico.

At a La Jicarita party

PHOTO BY JAKOB SCHILLER

Eric Shultz, Jake Kosek, Ike, David Correia, Kay Matthews, David's daughters Willa and Harper

Above: Willa, Harper, and David Correia;
Below: Jake Kosek, Jakob Schiller, Ike, Eric Shultz

Chapter One

La Raza Unida Party

Ike was born on New Year's Eve in 1946 and grew up in both the city of Española and La Madera, a rural norteño community. As a child he lived with his father, Antonio, who worked for 28 years for the Zia Company, a subcontractor of Los Alamos National Laboratory, and his mother, Louise, who worked 25 years as head cook for the Española schools. He much preferred La Madera, however, and after getting into some trouble at school, his parents sent him there to live with his grandparents. "The freedom of living in the country, going hunting, going fishing, going hiking . . . chasing cattle, raising animals, all that stuff was very interesting to me."[1] After his grandfather died when Ike was 16, he had to return to Española but worked for a while in the local forests hauling firewood, thinning, and logging.

Like many young men in northern New Mexico, however, he dropped out of high school, joined the army (or in Ike's case, the Marines), and was sent to Vietnam, and like many of these same men, his political education crystallized there. "Most of us went there believing what the government told us, that what they were doing over there was good and necessary, and most of us came back knowing that if they were lying to us over there they were lying to us here, too."[2]

Ike left for Vietnam when he was 17. Trained initially in Okinawa in parachute and scuba drills, then in the Philippines in jungle survival (trained there by a "Negrito," or Pygmy), he arrived in Vietnam as part of Operation Double Eagle Special Forces reconnaissance. These were the guys who were sent out to scout enemy territory for future operations and often ended up illegally in the DMZ (demilitarized zone), Laos, and Cambodia. After five months of extreme loss of life in his unit, he was sent back to Okinawa to recruit and re-train the unit, then back to Vietnam to finish out his tour. The previous iteration of his reconnaissance unit, while he was still in boot camp, was part of the covert operation in the Gulf of Tonkin that elicited confrontation by the Vietnamese and escalated American action into a state of war against North Vietnam. "It [boot camp] was racist as hell. I had never experienced racism before, frankly. I guess I can't say that there were some hard feelings in school with some of the Anglo teachers, there was some tension. I wasn't real aware of it, but it was nothing like the military."[3]

Ike in Vietnam, front row far left.

After his Vietnam tour ended in 1967 he spent five years traveling around the country, trying to adjust to being back in the States, trying to find his bearings. "I must have had 18 jobs all over the country, working for Los Alamos National Laboratory, in the Grants mine, up in Denver, and at the New Mexico Boys' School." But he couldn't deal with authority. He beat up the Boys' School administrator and almost beat up a Laboratory chemist. "I was not prepared for civilian life. I finally realized I had to be in the woods to survive." He came back to New Mexico, specifically Servilleta Plaza, and ended up working as a lumberjack for the multinational logging company Duke City Lumber in its sawmill in 1971, then for a subcontractor, Ramsey Logging

Company. Ramsey did all the logging for Duke City in the state except for the Vallecitos Federal Sustained Yield Unit (VFSYU), so until he later formed his own logging company, La Companía de Ocho, Ike never logged the VFSYU. This designated forestry unit, which will be discussed in detail later, was established by the US Forest Service in 1948 as compensation for the reduction of many rangeland permits on the 73,000 acres of the El Rito Ranger District of Carson National Forest. The stated purpose was to provide timber-related jobs to the local communities, but as Ike found out when he returned home from Vietnam, Duke City Lumber was the beneficiary, not the locals. "So I worked for Duke City quite a bit and that's where I started to get to know the different unions. One of the guys that was the union steward for the loggers ended up being my father-in-law. We would talk about the union and what they were supposed to be doing."[4] (Ike's father was injured on the job and forced to retire less than a year before the Zia Company union contract was signed and therefore unable to qualify for retirement.)

Ike quickly recognized that things weren't much better at home than they were in Vietnam. "When I got back from the military and I could see his [Rio Arriba County Sheriff and Democratic Party Chair, Emilio Naranjo] machine and his thugs and all that stuff, I thought to myself, well, shit, they ship me off ten thousand miles away to fight the dictators and I come home and we have a freaking dictator right here."[5] Ripe for action, he became involved with the La Raza Unida Party, a Chicano activist group originally organized in Texas but with a large membership in New Mexico. While Ike was still in Vietnam, most of the local attention had been focused on another northern New Mexico activist—Reies Lopez Tijerina (Tijerina is originally from Texas)—whose Alianza Federal de las Mercedes, leading the fight for the re-adjudication of Spanish land grant claims, had been involved in the infamous raid on the Rio Arriba County Courthouse in Tierra Amarilla. Ike explained that the two groups, the Alianza and La Raza, were involved in different issues, and that efforts to work together and revitalize the Alianza were not fruitful. After Tijerina came out of prison (he was convicted of destruction of federal property and assault on a federal officer and sentenced to two years' imprisonment), La Raza invited him to give a speech at one of their meetings, but as Ike put it, Tijerina was too interested in his own "cult of personality" to be supportive. "He shows up with a bunch of his people and he wants to talk. He wants to give the main speech. And I said no. You think we're all a bunch of pot heads [quoting Tijerina's rejection of a previous meeting with the State La Raza Unida Party] and you want to use us to push your agenda, then no, you are not speaking at this rally."[6]

PHOTO BY JAKOB SCHILLER

Reies Lopez Tijerina

Chicanos Associated Student Organization

The New Mexico chapter of La Raza Unida Party was founded by the Chicanos Associated Student Organization at Highland University in Las Vegas in 1971. While several of the founding students were influenced by the Socialist Labor Party, the group focused on local issues that affected the conservative, Catholic communities of San Miguel County: welfare rights, legal aid, food drives, job discrimination, and voting rights.

But they also took on the festering issue of police brutality against Chicanos in the San Miguel County, an issue that would be front and center for Ike when he became active in La Raza. A so-called "violence committee" maintained covert surveillance of the San Miguel County Sheriff's Posse, a paramilitary-like group of primarily Anglo ranchers who harassed La Raza members. In an interview with David Correia, author of *Properties of Violence: Law and Land Grant Struggle in Northern New Mexico*," La Raza member Juan Jose Peña said, "I was shot at in my car several times. I had bullet holes in my car. I had my house shot at. I had bullet holes in my back window that faces the alley. People shot at that. I had people throw rocks through the windshield of one of my cars."[7] The group also monitored the FBI, which they claimed tried to infiltrate the organization, with no success.

Another San Miguel County La Raza member, Manuel Archuleta, was a childhood friend of Ike's and recruited him to head a La Raza Unida Party in Rio Arriba County, Ike's home base. Ike said of Archuleta, "He had the greatest influence on me. I'd worked with Ramsey's [logging company] union a little bit, but he introduced me to the writings of people like community organizer Saul Alinsky and John L. Lewis [American labor organizer], which gave me a deep insight into working class America and the history of union organizing from the AFL to the CIO, and Rodolfo Acuña's *Occupied America: A History of Chicanos*, which had a big impact on me. The books radicalized me but Manuel's argument for a third party motivated me.

Naranjo's machine was very repressive, we couldn't go against him as a Democrat, so the only alternative was a third party."[8]

La Raza tried to convince other political groups in the state to work together as a coalition. "SWOP [Southwest Organizing Project] didn't want to deal with electoral politics, they're issue oriented. We thought they could be under our umbrella to pressure candidates but that didn't happen. Brown Berets could have been our army but here in Rio Arriba they were in a steep decline. I lived in Denver for a year to convince them that they could work with us to field candidates as part of their Crusade for Justice. But we never coalesced, although we continued to support each other."[9]

La Raza Unida demonstration

Rio Arriba County La Raza Unida Party

Emilio Naranjo

To achieve any success in dismantling the Naranjo machine in Rio Arriba County La Raza Unida had to get people elected to office. Early on they successfully elected two people to the school board in Gallina, one of the small villages on the north side of the Jemez Mountains. The party was less focused on the nationalistic state party and more focused on organizing at the community level. "Manuel and I broke apart later on, politically, after he joined Socialist Workers Party, I couldn't see that. We had to focus on what was happening in Rio Arriba County."[10]

What was happening in Rio Arriba County was systemic terror at the hands of the county sheriff, Emilio Naranjo, who was not only the sheriff but also chair of the Democratic Party and a former US Marshall and state senator. As such, he wielded unlimited power and abuse with his corrupt patronage.

As Ike explained it, "You couldn't be a public figure in New Mexico without his approval—the judges, the appeals court, the supreme court, the governor. You couldn't win an election without his approval. If you went against him he threatened your social security, food stamps, your job. How did he manage this? It was all patronage, starting at the lowest level, the schools. There were no independent school districts, just one superintendent for the entire county. That's why La Raza started running candidates for school board. A magistrate judge became one for life. Where there's a lot of domestic violence that ends up in court, they'd go to Emilio to get family members off. He also doled out money. The County used to rent offices from him. Dead people voted."[11]

Española, 1972 Photo by Tommy Nichols

David Correia says in his book *Property of Violence*, "When patronage failed to produce political results, Naranjo deployed an army of sheriff's deputies as enforcers." Ike again: "People were getting beat up every day. Deputies would stop a couple in a car, beat up the man, threaten the woman for a date that if she didn't agree to the man was going to jail. I think it was targeted, anyone he thought was independent, not kneeling at his altar. But it went beyond that as well. These deputies didn't understand politics but realized they had a free hand. It was chaos, lawlessness."[12] According to Correia, "Between April 1974 and May 1976 eighteen reported beatings or shootings by sheriff's deputies produced official complaints in the county. Dozens more, according to RUP [La Raza Unida] went unreported."

The *Rio Grande Sun*, the Española weekly newspaper, editorialized that the "unprovoked beatings, illegal property seizures, improper searches of private homes and downright terrorism are too numerous and well-documented to be ignored any longer."[13]

The abuse became even worse when Naranjo began to target La Raza as the group stepped up to challenge his authority. With an initial core group of about 20 to 25 members that grew to a hundred under Ike's leadership, La Raza began organizing against police brutality with petitions, protests, and rallies that brought people out by the hundreds. In June of 1975 Ike circulated a petition to dismiss Naranjo deputies who had arrested La Raza members the Valdez brothers on framed drug charges. The brothers were released but a family member was subsequently beaten in retaliation.

March in Española where Naranjo was hung in effigy.
Moises Morales, Ike, and Sammy Serna.

While Ike was based in the Española area, he soon met up with land grant and other activists further north in Canjilon and the Tierra Amarilla Valley who had organized community-based organizations to provide local services and also in response to increasing tourist development, e.g., a proposed airport in Ensenada, with a ski area in mind. These activists included Moises Morales, Pedro Archuleta, Andres Valdez, Susana Valdez, and Barbara Manzanares. Moises also introduced Ike to attorney Richard Rosenstock who would go on to defend Ike and other La Raza members as Naranjo turned up the heat on them. Rosenstock described Naranjo's deputies as a "paramilitary force." When he met Ike he was working at La Oficina de Ley, a legal aid office, one of the Tierra Amarilla Land Grant offices. The other organizations included: La Clinica del Pueblo del Rio Arriba, a free or low-cost medical clinic (Ike was the director from 1980 to 1982); La Cooperative Agricola (the Agricultural Cooperative), farming projects; and La Cooparación del Pueblo (The Unified People), economic projects (where Rosenstock first worked when he came to Tierra Amarilla from the Navajo Reservation).

According to Rosenstock, "La Raza Unida offered its support on the anti-tourism issue, solicited backing on their problems with the Sheriff's Department, and worked to show the people in the north that fighting the airport and the County Commission actually meant fighting Emilio Naranjo, as he exercised total control over all elected officials in Rio Arriba."[14]

In September of 1975 La Raza and supporters marched 95 miles from Tierra Amarilla, the Rio Arriba County seat in far northern New Mexico, to Santa Fe. At an Española rally on the way they hung Naranjo in effigy at the county offices, in front of the sheriff's office (housed in the Emilio Naranjo Building that Sheriff Naranjo rented to the county). Approximately 400 people at the rally chanted slogans directed at Naranjo and his deputies and speakers denounced the Naranjo dictatorship and police brutality. But it was the effigy, a dummy clothed in a suit with a sheriff's badge and an old Naranjo campaign poster that, according to Rosenstock, "was where La Raza Unida tactics changed from the politics of confrontation to the politics of provocation."[15] Ike had this to say. "The effigy thing did really flip him [Naranjo, who was present at the rally] out. . . This was local people whose parents he knew. There were connecting issues. Emilio knew that we had already made the linkages to the north of Española, all the way to T.A, [Tierra Amarilla] to the west, all the way to Gallina, to the east up into Truchas. So he knew that we were making a whole bunch of networks and that the people who were involved were locals. He couldn't write us off as agitators."[16]

In November of 1975, in response to the march and effigy hanging and after a bomb blew up a bar owned by a former undersheriff of Rio Arriba County, Naranjo let loose his deputies to harass La Cooperative officials and offices. Andres Valdez was taken into custody by four deputies and transported to the county jail in Tierra Amarilla for "questioning" on the bombing. When it was clear that Valdez had numerous witnesses to support his alibi, he was charged with another felony of possession of marijuana and arrested. Pedro Archuleta was arrested for possession of marijuana and possession of illegal weapons. Moises Morales was arrested for possession of marijuana and three misdemeanors and held for days without charge (Morales was one of the Alianza people who raided the Rio Arriba Courthouse). He claimed that Naranjo and his deputies put the marijuana in his truck to frame him (more on this later).

Naranjo's deputies then raided La Clinica del Pueblo del Rio Arriba, claiming that the basement was full of weapons. When they came up empty-handed they went next door to La Oficina de Ley, Rosenstock's office, and ransacked legal files. They later claimed that Morales had been an informant on the raids of La Clinica, but during a federal grand jury investigation of the sheriff's department for civil rights violations, a sheriff's deputy claimed Naranjo was going to frame Morales and Ike on drug charges and even put out orders for deputies to kill both men.

Ike stated unequivocally that Naranjo indeed put out a contract on his life.

"I grew up with Emilio's kids, especially in our first four years of school. I know them well. I love some of them—David, Joseph, Teresa, awesome people. My beef with Emilio at first wasn't personal, it was political. It got completely personal when he framed me on a drug charge. They raided my home when I wasn't there. I turned myself in but didn't spend any time in jail. They said I had heroin and pot, then after testing at the lab they said I had $79,000 of meth amphetamine. Where did Emilio get $79,000 of meth amphetamine? He thought it was heroin.

"When I was recruiting people for a La Raza rally an off-duty sheriff's deputy [Antonio Griego] challenged me to a fight. I was able to take his gun away from him and pistol-whipped him. I went to prison at the state pen to avoid getting killed at the local jail. They set a huge bond that my parents had to raise and it took a while to get me out, and they almost killed me in the state pen as well. I never ended up in court; they dropped the charges. The cop who I beat up later apologized and told me the whole story about how he was supposed to kill me."[17]

During this time Ike, in need of a job, started working with an outfit doing exploratory drilling in the Gallina area. He'd previously worked in the uranium mines in Milan, near Grants, and learned about the dangers involved, especially ground water contamination, but "I needed a job." When he found out that the company was going to be doing some drilling in the Hopewell Lake area, however, where many of the local streams originate—Tusas, Vallecitos, and Brazos rivers—he raised the issue with La Raza and they began organizing against any drilling. La Raza networked with various local environmental groups—including Taos Citizens Together—and Sam Hitt, who would go on to be a thorn in Ike's side as a member of Forest Guardians (Hitt also worked for La Clinica in Tierra Amarilla).

By 1976 Naranjo was under siege after La Raza Unida garnered 11 percent of the vote in county elections. While all of Naranjo's candidates were swept into office—Naranjo wasn't running for office, and both Ike and Moises Morales predictably lost their races for county commissioner—La Raza was encouraged by the percentage vote and that US Senator Joseph Montoya was defeated in his reelection bid. Montoya had long been Naranjo's mentor and supporter.

Taking Naranjo to Court

Lawsuits were filed by various parties, including two by Rosenstock, which were settled, and by Toney Anaya, the New Mexico Attorney General. Morales sued over the planting of drugs in his truck in November 1975. He settled his civil suit and called for Anaya to investigate what was done to him. Anaya did so, and Naranjo and his two deputies involved in that incident were charged with crimes. Naranjo was convicted of perjury and the other two pleaded to lesser charges. Emilio's conviction was overturned in a very controversial decision by the New Mexico Court of Appeals on the day before the state Democratic Convention that would have denied him chairmanship of the party as a convicted felon. Ike's suit was over the planting of methamphetamine in his home in 1976 by deputies. He sued Naranjo and the deputies involved and went to trial. Rosenstock and attorney Steve Farber represented him and the jury awarded Ike $56,000 in October 1978. Naranjo resigned as sheriff to become the county "law enforcement coordinator" who apparently had no duties. This was a new position that paid a higher salary than any elected position in the county, with no job description. Attorney General Anaya filed suit against the Rio Arriba County Commission and Naranjo asking state district court to invalidate Naranjo's position. The court upheld his hiring but forced him to pay back a month's salary that was paid to him before he actually began "work." According to the *Santa Fe New Mexican*, the ruling "shows there is little in state law to protect the public from political abuses in county hiring."[18]

Ike said of Naranjo, "He could have co-opted all of us if he'd just done some of the things we asked. Like taking control of his deputies. Clamping down on his crew would have stolen a lot of our thunder. But the more we attacked him the more he counterattacked and exacerbated the situation. We always knew what his response was going to be and we'd sue him and win. One of the lawsuits was during the winter of 1981, when five feet of snow blocked the road into La Clinica and we asked Naranjo to keep it open. He refused so we filed a lawsuit. Carol Miller, who succeeded me as director of La Clinica, settled the lawsuit."[19]

Miller described the action:

"Emilio's long time attorney Walter Kegel let down his guard with me in 1982 or 1983, soon after I followed in Ike's footsteps as the Executive Director of La Clinica. Kegel told me that of course the county wasn't going to fund the ambulance at La Clinica from the mill levy because Ike would have used it for La Raza Unida t-shirts. This conversation ended up being exactly how La Clinica finally won against Emilio. We now had proof that community health services were being denied in order to harm/prevent La Raza Unida members in leadership at La Clinica from being successful in their/our community organizing."[20] (Kegel subsequently made a complete political break with Naranjo.)

The lawsuit was settled with a large, one-time cash payment, and a share of the mill levy for healthcare was guaranteed to La Clinica for services in northern Rio Arriba.

Steve Farber, Ike, and Richard Rosenstock

Chapter Two

Back to the Woods

By the early 1980s Naranjo's power had been significantly diminished by all the lawsuits and eventual firings of his "military arm": the police and the sheriff's department. The county commission cut the sheriff's department to zero, leaving only a sheriff and an undersheriff, or what Ike called an "ineffective fighting force." Arthur Rodarte defeated Naranjo in both his last county commission race and state senator race. According to Ike, "He [Naranjo] could have retired at the top of his game, but he didn't do that. So he got beat. Once he got beat by Art Rodarte that was the beginning of the end."[21]

Moises Morales and Ike

The La Raza Unida Party in Rio Arriba disbanded in 1984 to support Jesse Jackson's presidential run. In order to send delegates to the convention members had to join the Democratic Party, but the new Democrats couldn't get the central committee to recognize them and get their delegates elected so they became the Democrats for Progress.

They hoped to then integrate with the mainstream party but then skipped that process and ran candidates on their own. They eventually started to collaborate with the mainstream party, but they worked separately and it fractured the Democratic Party. According to Ike, "If it hadn't been for La Raza there wouldn't have been a Democrats for Progress, which opened up who could run for office. The fear of retribution was no longer there. But the more radical ideas of La Raza are less integrated in politics today. The sense of alienation is still there."

When asked if the Democrats for Progress provided substantive change, Ike responded, "Yes, there's been substantive change and yet the more things change the more they stay the same. Now instead of one boss you have five or six, but there's the same kind of cronyism. The thing that has changed is that the people running the county are much more sophisticated. They're smarter and they cover their tracks better. They're not as arrogant as Naranjo was, although they're moving in that direction. It took Naranjo 30 years to become that arrogant; these guys have only been in power for 10 years and they're already running puppets for office. I do see improvements in the county roads. They've been paved or graveled and maintained. This kind of change is good but it's very limited. There's a lot of divisiveness and personal attacks that are totally unjustified. This divides the community and prevents any unity

Unknown, Ike, Moises Morales, Jesse Jackson, and Linda Pedro, below

of purpose. You want to get land grants back? You have to have unity of purpose. You want to maintain the Vallecitos Federal Sustained Yield Unit, you have to have unity of purpose. You want to effect policy at the state level, you have to have unity of purpose. This is why I'm not involved in politics anymore. Even the people I felt had the highest levels of integrity have fallen down to the basest levels of corruption."[22]

Linda Pedro and Ike

Another norteño activist who supported Jesse Jackson's Rainbow Coalition was Linda Pedro, a close comrade of Ike's since the La Raza Unida days. She and Ike met and became friends in 1977 when they teamed up to investigate the special education department at the Española schools that was siphoning off money into other programs. She gave a speech at the 1984 Democratic Convention in San Francisco for Jackson and challenged incumbent state senator Naranjo in the November general election. Naranjo won 7,345 to Linda's 355. She did all this after being severely injured in a 1966 car crash that left her a quadriplegic who fought for disability rights and was instrumental in helping create the Americans with Disability Act of 1990. She and Ike remained close friends and he regularly took her firewood to warm her house in Chimayó.

Once La Raza Unida Party disbanded Ike went back to the woods, just where he went when he returned from Vietnam. While he may not have been interested in getting involved in electoral politics during this period, he encountered an entirely different level of politics that played out over the next 20 years. To begin to understand what happened over that long, contested terrain readers need to know how the Vallecitos Federal Sustained Yield Unit set the stage for these battles.

Before 1947 the El Rito Ranger District of Carson National Forest was managed primarily for rangeland. Local permittees ran small-scale herds of goats, sheep, and cattle in the mountain pastures for mostly personal, subsistence use, a practice that originated with Spanish settlement in the sixteenth century and continues today on a much smaller scale. In the summer the fields were watered by the extensive acequia, or irrigation system, while the animal herds grazed the upper mountain ranges of primarily ponderosa pine with some spruce/fir, and were then brought back down to the fields for the winter. David Correia compiled figures that give an overview of this rangeland practice: "In 1935, 210 El Rito households farmed, on average, eight irrigated acres each, with one landowner irrigating 71 acres. While three families owned large herds, grazing a combined total of 3,260 sheep, and one family maintained 300 goats, most households maintained fewer than seven animals."[23]

But in 1947 the US Forest Service issued a study that claimed the livestock "caused surrounding national forest ranges to become depleted of vegetative cover to such an extent that a reduction in permitted grazing use is necessary." According to Correia, this was based on a survey of Southwest rangeland that suffered a severe drought from 1943 through the 1950s, although figures indicate that the El Rito Ranger District had "better than average precipitation patterns" and was not as depleted as other areas in the study.

The dice was rolled, however, and the Forest Service imposed grazing reductions on all Hispano small operators. Part of the agency's rationale, beyond the claim of ecosystem damage, was that this agropastoral way of life was responsible for the dire poverty in the district that needed to be addressed by switching the economic systems agricultural to timbering, dependent upon wage labor instead of subsistence labor. That post-war America was turning to this economy to provide jobs and housing across the country was a less touted but obvious rationale. As Correia put it: "The implementation of this policy coincided with the Forest Service post World War II effort to expand timber production by tying district budgets to timber output. It therefore served the interests of the Forest Service at the expense of the local population."

To underwrite this new economy the agency created the 73,600-acre Vallecitos Federal Sustained Yield Unit (VFSYU) in 1948, a special use designation to provide "the maximum feasible, permanent support to the Vallecitos community and nearby areas." Timber from the unit was to be cut and processed by a single designated operator who would establish a local sawmill and employ local residents. Carson National Forest set the annual timber yield at 1.5 million board feet (mmbf). In 1952, Jackson Lumber Company became the designated operator and immediately doubled the annual sustained yield to 3.5 mmbf. The company also asked for exemptions from the required 90 percent local labor standards, arguing that "competent men are not available locally." After Jackson left in 1957 the VFSYU was left without an operator for 15 years, causing the Forest Service to consider decommissioning it. Then, in 1972, instead of encouraging and helping facilitate local operators, the Forest Service designated Duke City Lumber, a subsidiary of the transnational Hansen Industries. According to Correia, "During its tenure, Duke City rarely maintained a labor force greater than 50 percent local, frequently circumvented labor standards, and ignored harvesting policies and covered up practices that caused erosion and water quality problems in the Unit. Yet the company continually lobbied for, and received, increases in the sustained yield of the 73,000-acre Unit."[24]

Vallecitos Association: "It's Not Sustainable"

This was the situation that drew Ike back into politics. Conflicts continually arose among the communities, the Forest Service, environmentalists, and Duke City Lumber. The local mill opened and closed with the fluctuations in the timber industry that was in trouble from too much indiscriminate cutting for too many years, the obsolescence of saw mills, less reliance on lumber products for building, and the exportation of timber. In response, local loggers and community members reformed an association to ensure that Vallecitos Federal Sustained Yield Unit employment requirements were met and the timber cut was sustainable. The association was first formed in the 1960s to ensure compliance with the local labor hiring practice. By the early 80s it was calling itself the Vallecitos Association, under Duke City, to force the Forest Service to manage the VFSYU to benefit the local community instead of the commercial operator.

As a member of the Vallecitos Association—and for a while its chair—Ike became involved in forest issues when the Carson Forest Plan, promulgated in 1985, set the new timber harvest levels for the VFSYU. "We told them right off that their ASQ [Allowable Sale Quantity] was not sustainable," Ike said. The Association believed that a volume of 3.5 million board feet (mmbf) was a reasonable cut in the Unit, while the Forest Plan called for 8 mmbf. At a 1985 public meeting, Hispano loggers repeated their concern not only for their jobs but also for the local forest ecology. As the president of the Association of local workers argued, "Increased logging and more roads will cause long-term ecological damage to the forest, reduce the sustained yield of the Unit, harm wildlife and adversely affect permittees." Local loggers and the Forest Service resolved the 1985 dispute regarding the potential doubling of the sustained yield when locals promised not to sue the Carson National Forest to stop the Forest Plan in return for a promise to reduce Duke City's annual yield to 5.5 mmbf and set aside 1 mmbf of saw timber and 1.1 mmbf of small forest products, such as vigas and latillas (small diameter logs used for beams and fences), for locally-owned operators. These allocations were to be put up and made available every year, for the life of the Forest Plan, so long as there was sufficient timber and other wood products within the Unit.

After the Forest Plan was implemented, Ike became involved with Madera Forest Products Association, which was trying to establish wood products businesses to replace the saw timber business. Started in 1988, the Association included membership of all the largely Hispano communities adjacent to the Vallecitos Federal Sustained Yield Unit: Vallecitos, Cañon Plaza, La Madera, Petaca, Las Tablas, and Servilleta Plaza. For a time, 50 people from these poor communities were employed by the local sawmill; Luis Torres, director of La Madera Forest Products, hoped that perhaps twice that number would be employed in economic development projects that included the manufacture of vigas, latillas, cabinets, and kiva ladders. According to Torres, "The Sustained Yield Unit has never evolved or really done anything for the progress of laborers. By now—40 years after the Unit was set aside—the loggers and mill workers should be in the management organization, not getting laid off when the mill shuts down. At some point, Duke City has to get out of here."[25]

Unfortunately, Madera Forest Products would fall victim to Forest Service policies that ran counter to rural development goals: no line-item budget for rural development; a bias towards large timber sales and against small sales and nonprofit contractors; lack of technical assistance and insensitivity to local conditions at the ranger district level; and national timber targets that overruled local decisions.

La Companía de Ocho

As a community member dependent upon logging for his livelihood, Ike soon realized that things were moving too slowly with the nonprofit Madera Forest Products to provide immediate relief and long-term stability for local loggers. Because the local mill in Vallecitos continued to open and close due to fluctuations of the timber market, the controversies surrounding the threatened New Mexico spotted owl, and the effects of years of over cutting in the Vallecitos Federal Sustained Yield Unit, Ike decided to organize his own for-profit company that could compete with Duke City Lumber for saw timber and whose members could have more control over their destinies. He felt that with a sustainable cut set by the Forest Service and the joint effort of Madera's wood products businesses and his company's saw timber business, the local industry could be viable and the community employed.

Along with Mike Peña, Patricio Valdez, Manuel Gurule, Steve Chavez, and Dennis Valdez, Ike approached the then Carson Forest Supervisor, John Bedell, about the possibility of starting a for-profit logging company that would be owned and operated by UFSYU residents and be eligible to receive the promised 1 mmbf of saw timber. Bedell saw this as fulfillment of the Federal Sustained Yield Management Act objectives and encouraged them to proceed. Eight members invested $1,000 each, using their homes and property as collateral, and with a loan guaranteed by all their combined land and possessions, bought enough equipment—loaders, skidders, trucks, bulldozers—to start La Companía de Ocho. "I'd like to see Duke City kicked out of the Carson and Santa Fe National Forests by 1995," Ike said. "This is another pendulum swing of the clock—from the small communities to the big corporations back to the small community mills. There will always be a need for timber management, without corporate timbering, and that's where we fit in."[26] Ike and members of the Vallecitos Association began to rewrite the Vallecitos Federal Sustained Yield Plan to reflect current needs and sustainable management.

PHOTO BY ERIC SHULTZ

Ike doing what he does best

The success of La Compania was limited by constant foot dragging on the part of the Forest Service. Bedell was transferred from the supervisor's office and subsequent supervisors subverted his efforts by failing to meet requirements. They allowed Duke City Lumber to purchase a timber sale and then sit on it until it was able to charge La Compania nearly double the stumpage as its subcontractor. Despite promising 1 mmbf/year to La Compania, the Forest Service offered for sale only 700,000 board feet in the ten years between 1986 and 1996.

According to Ike, "The first sale we bought ourselves was the Bolo sale. Here's where we first ran into problems with the Forest Service and realized what their attitude was. They were supposed to be offering a million board feet a year in small sales for local loggers, but they wouldn't sell us the Bolo One and Bolo Two sales until we filed a lawsuit. And when they were forced to offer it to us they charged us over three times as much per thousand board feet as they were charging Duke City. That demonstrated to us that they were trying to set us up to fail while trying to make themselves look good by saying they were making sales available to small operators. They were still biased in favor of Duke City because it's just as expensive to put up a small sale as it is a large sale and so they felt it wasn't worth it."[27]

PHOTO BY ERIC SHULTZ

A ponderosa pine, the object of so much controversy

The Forest Service also refused to recognize La Companía as an "approved operator" in the VFSYU because they hadn't shown "a bona fide intent in establishing a milling facility." This was contrary to the fact that La Companía had expressed its intent to either maintain the existing sawmill in Vallecitos or a small mill they had recently acquired near there. Carson Forest Supervisor Leonard Lucero claimed that they had to prove ownership of the mill and were therefore denied the right to contract for timber sales within the Unit, despite the fact that Duke City had operated in the Unit for 18 years without establishing a milling facility.

Similarly, despite frequent attempts by workers before 1985 to bring the tree theft perpetrated by Duke City subcontractors to Forest Service attention, no official investigation of these claims was ever undertaken. Yet after La Companía began operation, it was investigated many times for tree theft (more on this later).

PHOTO FROM ALAN LABB VIDEO

Ike with his beloved dog Thor

Chapter Three

The Lawsuits Begin

Felipito Timber Sale

In March of 1993 the US Fish and Wildlife Service listed the Mexican spotted owl as an endangered species. With this listing the threat of legal action hung over all timbering activity in northern New Mexico. In January of 1993 Mark and I, with our videographer friend Alan Labb, filmed Ike cutting wood in the Felipito Diversity Unit, the first sale in the Vallecitos Federal Sustained Yield Unit awarded to La Companía as a subcontractor of Duke City Lumber. The image of him casually wielding his chainsaw to lop off branches would do justice to any completed film about the mechanics of logging. In the background the noise of a skidder can be heard moving the cut logs around to be hauled away by truck. The 30-minute clip is personalized by Ike's black mastiff Thor, who tried to push onto Ike's lap once we got him to sit down and talk.

The Felipito was a 3.3 mmbf sale, one of three sales planned in the Felipito Diversity Unit, which spanned 16,800 acres. At the time of our interview La Companía had managed to cut 800,000 board feet in three months' time. Carson Forest Watch, an environmental organization based in the Peñasco area of northern New Mexico, appealed the Felipito timber sale in the fall of 1994 (Sam Hitt of Forest Guardians was an intervener in the appeal). According to Joanie Berde, essentially the one-person operator of Carson Forest Watch, the two main issues in the Felipito sale were spotted owl habitat in potential old growth and the depletion of renewable timber resources that would eventually affect the local community. Berde had already appealed the Alamo-Diner Sale, along with Forest Guardians, on her local Camino Real

Ranger District of Carson National Forest and lost, but would continue to work with Forest Guardians to appeal future VFSYU sales. When we interviewed Berde about her group's appeal of the Felipito, she mentioned that several other environmental groups had refused to join the Alamo-Diner appeal because they saw it as an "owl versus jobs" issue and didn't want to alienate local communities. Despite the fact that US Fish and Wildlife, the New Mexico Department of Game and Fish, and many of the local people were opposed to the size of the sale, Carson Forest Watch's appeal was denied, and a discretionary review by the Washington office of the US Forest Service was rejected.

Talking with Ike out in the woods, he told us the Felipito sale was the first time that environmentalists got involved in the management of the Felipito Diversity Unit: Forest Guardians, Carson Forest Watch, the National Audubon Society, and the Sierra Club. "In November of 1991, community people and environmentalists got together and came up with a seven-point plan where we agreed to give up a percentage of the Felipito sale if the Forest Service agreed to expand the Unit on the El Rito Ranger District. This scared the hell out of the Forest Service." Nothing came of that proposal, and the enviros proceeded with their appeals and lawsuits.

We also discussed the economic and environmental aspects of the Felipito sale. "All this hysteria about us destroying the area is crazy. There's a huge tract of old growth forest left. Our prescription is to harvest the Douglas fir and white fir, which have the infestations, and leave the ponderosa."

We asked if La Companía could make a living by cutting small diameter timber. "It's not economically feasible without access to the $5 million sawmill in Española owned by Duke City," Ike said. "Biologically, it's worth a discussion about what constitutes healthy old growth versus stands that are sick, and healthy potential old growth stands that should be left alone. But that gets lost in the hysteria about the spotted owl."

PHOTO FROM ALAN LABB VIDEO

Ike at Felipito sale

It wasn't just an impending appeal that was impacting the Felipito sale, though. It was the impending shut down of the sale from March through July for elk calving that was worrying Ike. "We had a meeting with [New Mexico] Game and Fish over elk calving and told them they need to amend the regulations that require a shutdown. Is elk an endangered species? They're the species that's really causing a certain amount of degradation in the woods. Does logging really disrupt the calving? They can just move off, away from the saws. La Companía has six to ten people working now, due to closures, instead of the usual 20. We have to finish cutting this unit by September of 1994. So far we've cut less than a million board feet. In order to stay viable, we need to bring in 5.5 mmbf. If we had access to milling, we might succeed."

The conversation segued to the ongoing confrontation between the Forest Service and La Companía over the agency's claim that 40 trees in the unit had been illegally cut.

"Trees in a timber sale that are accidentally cut are called 'quips,'" Ike told us. "It's uncommon and unusual for the Forest Service to bring in a federal investigator, like they did this time. But sometimes it's just an incident where trees fall into a meadow that the Forest Service wants to protect, or marked trees that are connected to or can't avoid being felled under other trees."

On the same videotape of Ike in the woods is footage of a community protest held in front of the El Rito Ranger Station after the Forest Service brought in the federal investigator about the 40 trees in the Felipito sale. Alan, Mark, and I went into the office to ask District Ranger Graciela Terrazas about the claims. She came to the counter and agreed to be filmed.

PHOTO FROM ALAN LABB VIDEO

El Rito District Ranger Graciela Terrazas

"Why did you turn this over to a federal investigator? Haven't there been other sales when unmarked trees were cut, either intentionally or accidentally?" I asked.

"There were 11 trees illegally cut last year, and 29 more this year, so we have an obligation to call an investigator. We didn't accuse anyone."

"But you spoke with Ike about it, right. He reported some of the trees to you, didn't he?"

"Yes, he did, but the Forest Service found most of the trees."

"But you call it 'timber theft.' Do you always use that language?"

"That happened only after it was publicized."

"Is Ike's claim that La Companía is being harassed valid?"

"No, but I have to acknowledge that trees were cut illegally . . ."

We then segued to a more general conversation about management of the Vallecitos Federal Sustained Yield Unit in general. We asked if she felt the mandates of the Unit, to help local people both financially and environmentally, were being met. She felt that to some extent it had succeeded in meeting that objective, and she didn't believe it had been over-logged.

"I came from other areas and was impressed when I came here because it's been vegetatively managed," she said. "We've implemented ecosystem management before many other forest areas in the country [Terrazas is an Hispana from southern New Mexico]. We'll be able to proceed with the biological evaluation of the New Mexico spotted owl listing as a threatened species, although there haven't been any sightings here. Our mandate is to manage the habitat."

Outside, Ike, Luis Torres of Madera Forest Products, Moises Morales, other La Companía members, and several dozen community people spoke about their struggles with the Forest Service as snow began to fall in large flakes. It was all conducted in Spanish. Terrazas came out and said she'd make a meeting room available if they'd like, but they turned her down, saying they were almost ready to break up. Several state cops drove up and shook hands with Ike and others, and then the politicos—Alex Atencio, the Rio Arriba County Republican Chair, and Greg Bemis, who was running for Congress against Democrat Bill Richardson—weighed in. They talked about the local people who need to make a living and how Senator Pete Domenici was fighting to keep cattle grazing and logging on public land.

PHOTO FROM ALAN LABB VIDEO

Luis Torres

Later I asked Ike what he thought about this kind of Republican support. This same question would arise when representatives of Duke City Lumber attended a demonstration in Santa Fe where norteños hung some members of the environmental community in effigy (more on this later). Ike's answer was always the same: "You know, it's a pain in the butt when you have to end up making a pact with the devil to survive. I hate it. But for me it's survival. If I have to go to bed with the devil to survive, then I'm going to do it. They're not alliances for life. They're alliances on one issue."

Ike later told us that after the demonstration the Forest Service pretty much dropped the tree theft investigation and left La Companía alone.

PHOTO FROM ALAN LABB VIDEO

At the El Rito demonstration

La Companía Sues the Forest Service

"Maybe it might have worked if we hadn't had so many outside problems: Duke City [Lumber] ripping us off, the Forest Service conspiring against us, and then the environmentalists shutting us down continuously. And finally, the community didn't support us. Some people formed a whole other logging group that didn't know a damn thing that was going on. Personal interests prevailed over the interests of the community, which was what La Companía was started for, to preserve the Sustained Yield Unit for the benefit of the community and provide meaningful jobs. It was a nice idea but it didn't work."[28]

The Felipito appeal dragged on and La Companía, stymied by environmentalists, Duke City, and the Forest Service, entered arbitration over the fulfillment of contractual obligations with Duke City. Hired to log two sales, the Valle Grande and Borracho, La Companía claimed that the proper payments for cut timber were not made and it was being cheated at the weigh station. The actual volume of logs that were processed by La Companía exceeded the volume estimated by Duke City's scaling. A second subject of disagreement was reimbursement for La Companía's delays and losses incurred when operations could not be conducted on the timber sale areas because the roads were not in adequate condition for hauling. Construction of the roads was sole responsibility of Duke City. After arbitration, a settlement was reached, and Duke City agreed to pay La Compañía $200,000 to compensate for the damages incurred.

Ike and Richard Rosenstock

Then, in 1994 La Companía filed a lawsuit against the US Forest Service for the agency's "practiced and demonstrated patterns of discrimination and retaliatory conduct." The lawsuit also highlighted its failure to meet its fiduciary agreement in the Vallecitos Federal Sustained Yield Unit, for its failure to implement the Carson Forest Plan, and for its long-term lack of commitment to sustainable communities. Joined by Madera Forest Products and the individuals Manuel Gurule, Steve Chavez, Dennis Valdez, and Ike, the complaint named Mike Espy, Secretary of Agriculture; Larry Henson, the Regional Forester; two Carson Forest Supervisors, Leonard Lindquist and Leonard Lucero; the Taos District Timber Specialist Stet Edmonds; and the El Rito District Ranger Graciela Terrazas. Richard Rosenstock and several other attorneys represented La Companía de Ocho, and Northern New Mexico Legal Services (or Legal Aid) represented Madera Forest Products.

The plaintiffs requested 21 judgments in the lawsuit (abbreviated below):

1. La Companía is approved as a responsible operator within the VFSYU without having to own a sawmill as long as its product is processed within the Unit.
2. The Forest Service is required to offer 1.0 mmbf of sawtimber to approved local operators.
3. The Forest Service is required to offer 1.7 mmbf to La Companía to cover the period from 1990 through 1993.
4. The Forest Service is required to offer 500 mbf to the individual plaintiffs to cover the period of 1993.
5. An injunction requiring the Defendants to offer 5.5 mmbf for sale to all approved operators within the Unit to cover the years from 1986 through 1992.
6. An injunction requiring the Forest Service to offer former units 8 and 9 of the Felipito sale to the plaintiffs at the same stumpage price the rest of the sale was purchased by Duke City in 1992.

Other judgments included road building issues, elk calving, 1,684 mbf of firewood for sale to Madera Forest Products and other approved operators, compensatory damages, punitive damages, and attorney fees and costs.

Ike summarized the lawsuit this way: "At the very minimum the Forest Service needs to live up to the *1968 management policy* (emphasis added) and that means getting rid of Duke City."[29]

The "1968 management policy" Ike was referring to is what is known as the Hassell Report, or "The People of Northern New Mexico and the National Forests," written by M.J Hassell in 1968. This report was made at the request of then US Forest Service Region Three Forester, William D. Hurst, "to determine possible ways of making the resources of the National Forests in northern New Mexico and the work they generate contribute more effectively to the people who reside there.” In his letter releasing the report to forest supervisors and district rangers in 1972, Hurst wrote: “First, the uniqueness and value of Spanish American and Indian cultures in the Southwest must be recognized and efforts of the Forest Service must be directed toward their preservation. These cultures should be considered ‘resources’ in much the same sense as Wilderness is considered a resource with Forest Service programs and plans made compatible with their future well-being and continuance.”

This is the paragraph that is most often cited by norteños when contesting Forest Service policy and actions. Today, it sounds both progressive, in its recognition that the people of northern New Mexico are a “resource,” and somewhat patronizing in its use of the term “preservation,” as if this resource is not alive and well and constantly in flux. What Ike, and many others have advocated, is that because of this cultural history the forests of el norte are unique and need to be managed with this foremost in mind.

Hassell states at the outset of his report that the document is not the result of an in-depth study and analysis but rather “a collection of ideas” that he believed would best serve the people of el norte. They include range management, sanitary landfills, recreational development, timber marketing, road development, technical engineering assistance, fire control, watershed restoration, employment opportunities, and training and education. But the failure of the Forest Service to build trust with the people, to overcome what Hassell describes as the “cognitive dissonance” between what the people expect of the Forest Service and what it actually delivers, brings us to the 1994 lawsuit.

In February of 1996 the lawsuit was settled when the Forest Service agreed to compensate La Companía in several ways and to adjust its management policies in the Vallecitos Federal Sustained Yield Unit. These included: 1) guarantee that a minimum of 28 percent of the timber budget is spent on the El Rito Ranger District [where the Unit is located]; 2) design sales on the Unit to minimize the impact caused by elk calving restrictions; 3) hold public meetings twice a year to provide the schedule of timber sales on the Unit for the next six months, with their estimated value, location, species of trees, etc.; 4) guarantee La Companía 75 percent of the sawtimber from the La Manga timber sale and 80 percent of the sawtimber from the Agua/Caballos timber sale without competitive bidding; 5) write an amendment to the Carson Forest Plan which stipulates that timber sales on the Unit will be open to competitive bidding rather than a designated operator [previously Duke City Lumber]; 6) provide $40,000 in compensation to La Companía; and 7) issue a 10-year special use construction permit if La Companía wishes to build a primary processing facility in the Unit.

"When we won against the Forest Service," Ike said, "they had to give the communities all of La Manga [timber sale] because there wasn't any other timber. So in essence we kicked Duke City out of the Sustained Yield Unit. That's something the environmentalists can't take credit for although they try to. And they get funded because of it."

La Manga Timber Sale

But La Companía hit another brick wall as soon as the 2.1 mmbf La Manga Jo sale was released in 1995. It was immediately appealed by Forest Guardians, Carson Forest Watch, and Forest Conservation Council, claiming the Forest Service was breaking the law by offering a sale in Mexican spotted owl habitat. After settling its lawsuit with the Forest Service, La Companía intervened in the subsequent La Manga lawsuit claiming economic interests. The fight over La Manga would linger for three years, exacerbated by the Mexican spotted owl lawsuit, filed by the same New Mexico environmentalists and others in Arizona, which shut down US Forest Service Region Three for 18 months.

In the first issue of *La Jicarita*, January 1996, we interviewed Ike about the lawsuits and the November 24, 1995 protest demonstration in Santa Fe where Ike, along with a newly formed group of norteños called La Herencia del Norteños Unidos, hung Sam Hitt of Forest Guardians and John Talberth of Forest Conservation Council in effigy. We started by asking him if he still believed that the Forest Service was primarily responsible for the mismanagement of the forests of northern New Mexico after targeting the environmentalists at the demonstration in Santa Fe. He responded:

"I still feel that way. However, the reason we targeted the environmentalists is because we consider them to be interlopers. If they want to have a productive dialogue over the management of the forests, what they should do is come to the community groups that are struggling with the Forest Service, form coalitions with them, and serve as consultants instead of imposing their will or their ideas on the community. Now most of these people aren't from here, they want these forests to be managed like the forests in Oregon, Washington, or Idaho, and these are just different forests. They're managed differently for specific reasons. The 1968 forest report [Hassell Report] outlines these reasons."

We brought up the fact that representatives of Duke City Lumber attended the demonstration (mentioned previously in the Felipito sale chapter) and asked Ike how he felt about it.

"I anticipated that they would attend. I feel that they're just as welcome as anybody else. They're affected by what these people are doing. They have the right to assemble just like I do, just like the Rainbows do. I didn't send out invitations to them. You know, it's a pain in the butt when you have to end up making a pact with the devil to survive. I hate it. But for me it's survival. If I have to go to bed with the devil to survive, then I'm going to do it. They're not alliances for life. They're alliances on one issue."

We then asked what he thought motivated the environmentalists to pursue these lawsuits.

"I don't think they're environmentalists. I think they're preservationists. They would like to see all the forests closed down completely to all human entry; that includes ski areas, hunting and fishing, cross-country skiing, camping. I don't think they want any people in any national forest, period. They just want nature to take its course. I see these people as cultists, quite frankly. They have formed this cult called deep ecology, and to me, most cults are just not rational. I don't think it's possible to do what they want to do, but they're so idealistic and tunnel-visioned. And in the process they're disrupting a hell of a lot of lives . . . In our negotiations with the environmentalists on the La Manga timber sale we said, let's hold in abeyance the 500 acres of old growth and negotiate on that, but release the rest of it, because the rest of it is not in old growth. That way La Companía and the community can get back to work with the remaining 3.5 million board feet. They didn't want to talk. Which led us to believe that they didn't want any cutting. That's the bottom line."

We then talked about La Companía's attempt to acquire the Vallecitos sawmill, which had been such a contentious issue with the Forest Service. Ike told us that La Companía had already sent an offer of purchase to Duke City for the sawmill, which they had just shut down.

"As part of the settlement negotiations on our lawsuit, the Forest Service had said it would give us a grant under the Community Development Grant program for up to $200,000, specifically for the purchase of the sawmill. Or if Duke City didn't want to sell, the Forest Service would make land available to us on a special use permit so we could use that $200,000 to purchase our own milling equipment. The Forest Service reneged on that agreement. But we've had offers from other foundations for money to buy the mill. I also think the mill in Española should be bought by all the logging contractors who have been working for Duke City. I view the Vallecitos Federal Sustained Yield Unit as a microcosm of the big picture. Duke City wants 7 million board feet out of the unit; we're saying 3.5 is OK. They say they need 40 million board feet out of the Carson for the Española mill, we're saying 10. If we do value-added work and the profits come to the community, we don't need as much volume as Duke City needs. Some of these loggers are making a decent living, but they're still getting ripped off. Duke City is the one making the killing. So if all the logging contractors and the small sawmill owners were to get together and buy Duke City out, we could then compromise on a lower level of volume, and we could log it together and mill it together, market it together, and reap the benefits together."

The sawmill continued to be a stumbling block for La Companía as other actors jumped into the fray. Then Congressman Bill Richardson's office announced that Duke City Lumber had turned over its Vallecitos Lumber Mill to La Herencia del Norteños Unidos, a coalition of groups that included La Madera Forest Products, the rural electric co-op, cattlemen's associations, La Companía de Ocho, and Las Comunidades, a recently organized community association. While members of La Herencia gave final approval to the transfer agreement on April 11 of 1996, the group didn't know who would actually operate the mill once it became the owner. Ike was not happy with the deal.

"The Vallecitos mill should have unquestionably gone to the Vallecitos Association, which represents the Vallecitos Federal Sustained Yield Unit. And the timber available to the mill must be logged in the Vallecitos Unit. No outside loggers can come in and log in the Vallecitos,"[30] Ike said. He went on to explain that because of La Companía's recent settlement with the Forest Service, guaranteeing La Companía 75 percent and 80 percent of the next two logging units in the VFSYU, his company was the only one that could provide the mill with timber. If the Vallecitos Association owned the mill, La Companía would be able to log and mill the timber and keep it all within the Unit. Under La Herencia ownership La Companía would have to lease the mill at fair market value.

Ike further claimed that La Companía was not involved in the final negotiations between Duke City, Richardson's office, and La Herencia, and that some of the other member groups were opposed to the transfer of the mill to La Herencia as well. He claimed that Las Comunidades, the other group that had expressed interest in operating the mill, would "kill themselves" if they tried to run the mill because they had neither the timber nor the expertise.

Ike already had a long-standing antipathy towards Richardson, often expressed publicly, and had this to say about the negotiations over the sawmill.

"Richardson said we needed a non-profit to accept the donation of the mill and we told him we had one, Madera Forest Products. He said, no no no, we needed another one, so he created La Herencia, which only acted as a pass-through and essentially doesn't even exist today. La Herencia then donated the mill to another non-profit start-up, Las Comunidades, which got a $200,000 grant from the Department of Energy to retool the mill. This took advantage of a division in the community and essentially meant that control of the mill would be taken away from La Companía, the only operator that was logging in the Unit. This forced us to spend our loan money on equipment that already existed at the mill; another saw, another loader, and other costly tools. With that money we could have bought a kiln drier, a planer moulder, and a chipper. Then we would have had the entire component we needed to sell the lumber we harvested at top dollar. Because of the state construction codes you have to have dried and planed lumber to sell to contractors.

"Today, the mill is just sitting there, they've never used it. In fact, there's a stack of logs that they bought from another local contractor that has never been milled. So those trees are rotting at the sawmill, just like the ones in the woods. I blame Bill Richardson for the trees left in the woods, for the trees rotting at the sawmill, and I blame him for the destruction of La Companía. I also think he defrauded the taxpayers because the $200,000 was never used to retool the mill. I'd also like to know what kind of tax break Duke City got for giving the mill to La Herencia."

The La Manga lawsuit was fought in New Mexico Federal Court, Arizona Federal Court, and the Court of Appeals in San Francisco, forcing, along with the spotted owl lawsuit and injunction (filed in 1995, discussed in the next chapter), La Companía out of the woods for almost three years.

A Walk in the Woods

Over the weekend of August 2-4, 1996, Forest Conservation Council and Forest Guardians hosted a campout at the La Manga timber sale site. According to spokespersons for the groups, the purpose of the campout was to show the proposed timber sale to the public and discuss the issues regarding the future of the area. Over the course of the three days, the groups also sponsored workshops on tree sitting, nonviolence, mountain biking, and mushroom and bird identification. According to Sam Hitt of Forest Guardians, local area loggers, including members of La Companía de Ocho, interveners in the La Manga lawsuit, were also invited to visit the camp to discuss the issues.

The norteños chose to stage their own gathering, however, and on Friday, hung Sam Hitt and John Talberth in effigy from trees along Forest Road 274, which leads to the timber sale. According to Ike, the locals felt that the environmentalists' gathering was "provocative" and counter-productive, as all the parties were still involved in legal negotiations over the sale.

John Talberth Effigy

I visited the gathering on Saturday afternoon to interview the concerned parties. The dummies still hung from the trees, accompanied by numerous signs along the route: "It's not the owl, stupid, it's your way of life and culture that's at stake;" and "Enviro-maniacs are the dregs of the 1960-70s hippie movement . . . Go Home!" The norteños were camped alongside the road about a mile before the environmental sentries who manned the entrance to their gathering. People entering the environmentalists' site had to identify themselves and were then given directions along the bumpy, rained-slicked road into the campsite.

When I arrived, small groups were already out hiking several of the timber sale cutting units. Approximately sixty people were in attendance, including an activist group from San Luis, Colorado, called La Sierra.

Their representative, Praxedis Ortega, a native rancher and farmer, had been involved in that community's struggle to regain access and ownership of their former common lands in the Culebra Peak area of the Sangre de Cristo Mountains, then owned by the Taylor family (descendants of Zachary Taylor, former US President) of North Carolina. The area was being logged by Stone Forest Industries, and according to Ortega, the logging activity was threatening the health of the watershed. Ortega and his friends from Colorado attended the New Mexico gathering because "we have to rescue the last of the ancient forests." (The land grant heirs eventually won access to the ranch in 2002).

I met up with Hitt on a walk through the cutting unit. He denied that the gathering was meant to be "provocative." When asked if there was any room for compromise with La Companía towards resolving the lawsuit, he responded: "This stand of forest must be protected," and that La Companía's insistence on cutting a certain percentage of the large ponderosa pines in the sale was "culturally irresponsible."

I asked if this might be a good time to make a concerted effort to form a coalition with the loggers, as the Forest Service was threatening to reduce the number of board feet that will be available to La

Companía, and a united effort on the part of the environmentalists and loggers could result in a better management plan for future sales. Hitt responded that while he thought coalitions were important, in this instance there was too much cultural antagonism, too many differences in the levels of knowledge between the two groups, too much media overplay, and too much Forest Service involvement.

I suggested that perhaps he and his group were the ones being "culturally irresponsible." The small, rural communities of northern New Mexico are the last bastion of defense against the suburbanization and urbanization of the area, and environmentalists and norteños must work together to ensure that these communities remain economically and culturally viable. While Hitt admitted that this was indeed a threat, he expressed hope that land use plans, like the one being developed in Rio Arriba County, would be able to halt the threat of development. "My bottom line is that these old growth pines will not be cut."

While walking the cutting unit, which seemed to be a healthy mix of large- and small-diameter trees with tall, underlying grass, one of the environmentalists pointed out a snag with a goshawk nest at the top, a threatened species. Apparently, this nesting site was discovered after the Environmental Impact Statement was completed by the Forest Service and was not identified in that document.

On my way out to visit the norteño gathering, Hitt met me at the security site and made an offer: If Ike and the others would agree to take down the effigies, he and some of the environmentalists would be willing to visit their campsite to discuss the issues. I delivered the message to Ike, who immediately agreed to take down the dummies and said any of the environmentalists who wanted to come would be welcome. I then turned around and drove back to the environmentalists' security site and delivered the message to Hitt. An hour later about eight of the environmentalists arrived at the norteño camp, where Hitt, Ike, and some of the others, including Max Córdova, President of the Truchas Land Grant, sat in camp chairs and talked for about 45 minutes. While there was a lot of finger-pointing, name-calling, and not much agreement on anything, once the more formal conversation between the two camps was over, Hitt and some of his fellow environmentalists stayed around and engaged in informal conversations with the rest of the norteños.

PHOTO BY ERIC SHULTZ

Ike and Sam seated across from each other

When I later asked Ike if he thought the meeting had been worthwhile, he responded, "Actually, I thought it was productive. While we're only 16 days away from a settlement conference on the La Manga lawsuit, and it's too late to do anything on an informal level about that, I think it set the stage for some things that will come up in the future. And I think it was important that Sam talked to some of the others here, not just me, a wild-eyed crazy activist, to see what even a two-month layoff means to working people. We know we have to diversify beyond just sawtimber, but until we have the money to buy things like bent lamination, let Sam put his money where his mouth is and buy it for us; we need to go to work."

PHOTO BY ERIC SHULTZ

Ike at campsite

As he had stated in previous interviews, he stressed that this whole breakdown could have been avoided if the environmentalists had agreed to release the La Manga sale, except for the 500 acres of old growth, and negotiate with the loggers on how to manage that, or trade it for another potential old growth area. As for Hitt's bottom line that no large trees should be cut, period, Ike responded that probably very few of the trees that Hitt pointed out to us would actually be harvested.

He reiterated that while it was too late for any negotiations on the La Manga sale outside the courtroom, he thought it was still possible for these groups to form a coalition to discuss future issues. "Let's get together over a period of time so that we can work together to pressure the Forest Service. I still view the Forest Service as an army of occupation, occupying northern New Mexico with economic and political force rather than with guns. I'm harsher with them than I am with Sam. But he can no longer portray himself as David fighting Goliath, out to save the poor people against the corporate giant. He's now become Goliath."

In September of 1996, a federal judge, Edwin Mechem, ordered the Forest Service to offer the La Manga sale to La Companía, stating that the injunction halting all logging in US Forest Service Region Three (discussed in the next chapter) did not apply to La Manga. The environmentalists immediately went to the judge and asked for a stay on his decision until there was clarification as to whether the logging injunction applied to the sale.

Mexican Spotted Owl Lawsuit

The Mexican spotted owl lawsuit alleged that the US Forest Service Region Three had failed to look at the cumulative impacts of logging on the Mexican spotted owl in planning its timber program. By submitting its timber projects to the US Fish and Wildlife Service on a project-by-project basis rather than considering the forest as a whole or forest plans as a whole, the suit claimed that the Forest Service had violated the Endangered Species Act. In August of 1995, a federal judge in Arizona issued an injunction that halted all logging on the affected forests.

The injunction caused hardship throughout the region and contentious settlement negotiations eventually brought it to a close 18 months later.[31] The settlement placed several restrictions on the Carson National Forest. First, no dead and down wood in the forest could be gathered in the owl's habitat and in sensitive streamside zones. Maps were drawn up showing the areas where wood gathering was permitted and mailed to everyone who had obtained a firewood permit. According to the environmentalists, critical owl habitat amounted to less than a third of the area within a 20-mile radius of Peñasco, on the Camino Real Ranger District. Second, the only cutting allowed of green trees was from marked areas. Standing dead piñon and juniper could be cut outside critical habitat, while ponderosa pine could not.

For many years (since the early 1970s, with only a few restrictions in place) the Carson had an unrestricted firewood gathering policy that allowed for free wood gathering anywhere on the forest and for the cutting of standing dead trees. According to Joanie Berde of Carson Forest Watch, the Forest Service recognized a problem with this policy due to declining populations of songbirds and other wildlife that depend on dead and down trees for habitat. While Berde and other environmentalists agreed that there needed to be reasonable restrictions on the firewood policy, they felt the Forest Service should have done it the right way with public input and by amending the Carson Forest Plan. They also accused the Forest Service of not offering enough thinning sales in low-impact areas for people to cut green wood instead of emphasizing large commercial sales. (The Camino Real Ranger District did establish seven thinning areas near Peñasco to supply firewood for the 1996 season.) Ike was upset by the negotiations because he felt they not only failed to address the needs of the Vallecitos community, which is supposed to benefit from the Vallecitos Federal Sustained Yield Unit, but that it prevented him and his coworkers in La Companía from getting back to work.

PHOTO BY ERIC SHULTZ

Max Córdova on right

More controversy developed when the Truchas Land Grant declared that because of firewood restrictions many people in the village of Truchas, on the Camino Ranger District, did not have enough wood to get through the winter. Because the Truchas Land Grant is still extant and well organized, this claim immediately garnered huge media attention, and soon reporters from *The New York Times*, *Los Angeles Times*, CBS, and NBC were winding their way up the precipitous canyon highway to picturesque Truchas (where John Nichol's *Milagro Bean Field War* was made into a movie by Robert Redford) to interview Max Córdova, president of the land grant, and the various villagers who had run out of firewood. It made a compelling story—the last vestiges of a rural life being eclipsed by the twentieth century, with villagers suffering their final defeat at the hands of capricious environmentalists taking wood out of their stoves and food out of their mouths.

Everyone had a different take on what caused the firewood shortage or if there even *was* a firewood shortage. William deBuys, author and historian, wrote an editorial saying, "The Arizona decision did not create the shortage of dead and down fuelwood in the Truchas area, but it certainly intensified it and brought it to the front page." Sam Hitt of Forest Guardians declared, "It's unbelievable [around Truchas]. You go into the forest and it's like Mexico or third world countries in Asia. There's not a stick left. It's creating huge problems for the wildlife. All 40 species of resident songbirds are in decline." Both agreed that there was a more severe problem in Truchas because it sits right at the edge of the national forest, above the high desert of the Española Valley, and sees more wood gatherers from valley residents in Córdova, Chimayó, and Española than do the villages higher in the mountains. The previous fall the Forest Service had opened up a greenwood area for firewood gathering just down the road from Truchas, but designated a fairly limited number of cords that could be cut. Forest Guardians and Forest Conservation Council responded to the Truchas community by collecting money from donations and buying cords of wood from the Chama area that were hauled to Truchas and cut and split on site.

Despite all the ranting and raving, there was obviously some common ground that needed to bind both the environmentalists and community activists in a united front. While many accusations of "racism" were hurled about in the heat of the argument—and there is validity to this claim—the real issue here was class: making the distinction between corporate greed and sustainable, locally based resource needs. Both Berde and Ike repeatedly called for getting rid of Duke City (a buy-out changed ownership of Duke City Lumber from Hansen Industries, a multi-national corporation, to Idaho Timber Corporation). The lawsuit filed by La Companía and the Vallecitos Association had tried to do just that. Ike had said all along that if Duke City were out of the equation, if La Companía had the funds to buy the sawmill in Vallecitos, and a consortium of small loggers could buy the mill in Española, much less timber would be taken out of the Vallecitos Federal Sustained Yield Unit and the forest as a whole.

Berde and other environmentalists agreed that the Forest Service should start offering smaller sales that would benefit the small operators, but maintained a hard line about the cutting of any amount of old growth—i.e., certain diameter trees—within the VFSYU or anywhere on the Carson. Berde insisted that the environmentalists and Ike shouldn't be arguing about the La Manga timber sale, that other potential sales on the Unit could provide enough sawtimber from smaller dimension trees than in La Manga. Ike, however, said that any sale they might come up with would result in the same conflict—there were large trees in all of the areas except those that had been timbered within the last thirty years, and these were not yet ready for reentry. These two groups needed to sit down together because La Companía had settled its lawsuit with the Forest Service that guaranteed sawtimber from La Manga. But over the course of the next year, as a negotiated settlement of the environmentalists' lawsuit failed time and time again, there would be no substantive dialogue between environmental groups like Forest Guardians and Carson Forest Watch and the norteño communities.

Mediation: Environmentalists/Communities/Forest Service

A few weeks after the campout at La Manga, on Sunday, August 25, fifty people met at the Oñate Center north of Española for what was called a teach-in, but was in reality a four-hour brainstorming session.[32] With the statue of Juan de Oñate standing sentinel outside, fifty people probed, questioned, and analyzed the "bad dynamic" that existed between the environmental community and the people whose livelihood depended upon the use of public lands in northern New Mexico. Organized by Ike and Chellis Glendinning, a writer and activist from Chimayó, attendance was diverse: Green Party members from Rio Arriba, Taos, and Santa Fe counties; New Mexico Public Interest Group from Albuquerque; Jan-Willem Jansens of Forest Trust; Maria Varela of Los Ganados del Valle; George Grossman of the Sierra Club; Tony Povilitis of the Greater San Juan Coalition; Janice Varela of La Gente del Rio Pecos; Donna House, Native American activist; Richard Rosenstock, attorney for La Companía de Ocho; Santiago Juarez and Moises Morales, longtime community activists; and various community members from Placitas, Ojo Caliente, Tierra Amarilla, Los Alamos, and Antonito, in Colorado.

In her opening remarks, Glendinning set the tone. "We are living in an imperialist society where we are treating our Chicano neighbors as our fathers did and their fathers before them." According to Glendinning, the bad dynamic that had been occurring was the result of four behavior patterns: 1) a need to control; 2) a life lived too fast, where the quality of attention is lost; 3) blaming the recipients of colonization instead of the perpetrators; and 4) deifying conflict, where "in your face" politics is promoted as the only way to accomplish anything. To break down these patterns, she said, "we of the dominant culture need to listen and learn."

Ike moderated the remainder of the meeting, stating that his purpose in participating in this dialogue and in all his activism was to promote Chicano culture and sovereignty. In a brief synopsis of local history, he described how Hispanos went from being subjects of Spain to those of the United States, with a brief interlude under Mexican control. Now his "isolated culture" was caught between corporations that want to rape the land, corporations that want to take the land for recreation, and government agencies "that treat us like rats in a lab." He also pointed out that because of the continued loss of land—in the old days no one would have built a house below an acequia—his people have become increasingly dependent upon timber resources.

The abuse of the Endangered Species Act (ESA) was a recurrent theme throughout the day. Richard Rosenstock said it was the misuse of the ESA that was causing hardships in northern New Mexico by limiting grazing and timbering. He explained that the federal court injunction prohibiting all commercial logging in northern New Mexico had severely impacted the lives of norteños because "that's [logging] the only game in town right now."

Maria Varela of Los Ganados del Valle, a sheep and wool cooperative in the Tierra Amarilla area, told the group, "We need to be aware that the Forest Guardians has filed suit to enjoin grazing on the forests of northern New Mexico. While none of us has all the answers, some of the traditions that were here are based on sustainability learned over thousands of years. There is a role grazing can play in the environmental balance."

Donna House, a Native American activist from Española, supported Varela's position. "This is a return of the battle Los Ganados fought eight years ago to find grazing land for their sheep. There is still a grave lack of understanding of the economics of land-based communities." She stated that the misuse of the Endangered Species Act has harmed Native American communities and that a San Ildefonso man was being prosecuted for religious use in violation of the act.

Tony Povilitis of Pecos, a member of the Greater San Juan Coalition, gave an overview of the owl's range, from northern Mexico north along the edge of the Sangre de Cristo range and into Colorado, citing it as a "friend who can help us" because of its status as an indicator species. He accused Rosenstock of sounding like an industry oilman, insisting that an endangered species had never been sighted to clear the way for exploiting a resource.

There was more verbal sparring back and forth, with Rosenstock responding, "The owl is not a friend to the people of northern New Mexico who are out of work," and Povilitis asking not to be pigeonholed with the people who are abusing the ESA and are becoming a part of the imperialist culture.

Ike attempted to quiet tempers by explaining that the Vallecitos area is on the fringe of owl habitat, and the "abuse of discretion" by the Forest Service has caused economic hardship in the area.

Sam Hitt of Forest Guardians and John Talberth of Forest Conservation Council were not invited to the gathering, but their names frequently came up in discussion. Varela accused both of "smashing" La Madera Forest Products by refusing to release sales it needed to operate. If environmentalists in the room didn't want to be "tarred with the broad brush" of Hitt and Talberth's actions, she said, they should stop the spread of misinformation by being more vocal. Rosenstock added that in his opinion Hitt and Talberth had "usurped" the environmentalists' voice and power. The ensuing exchange between environmentalists and norteños about who spoke for the environmental movement revealed that the bad dynamic was far from being resolved. Earlier in the dialogue Maria Varela stated, "I get suspicious of these democracies where urban environmentalists overspeak and outvote us. Until you walk in our moccasins, don't preach to us about what is sustainable." Santiago Juarez added to that sentiment when he said, "The people in Vallecitos fought for years against Duke

City and against clear-cuts, before Forest Guardians were ever there. Local communities are not dupes."

A second mediation session was held the following October with many of the same participants as well as Max Córdova, president of the Truchas Land Grant. This time, however, the discussion largely focused on the US Forest Service that had failed to protect both local communities and public land resources.

Chellis Glendinning, Max Córdova, Ike

Much of the conversation centered on the firewood crisis that occurred in the Truchas area the previous year and what should be done to prevent a recurrence. Córdova explained that land grant representatives met 14 times with environmental groups, including Forest Guardians and Forest Conservation Council, to devise a plan to ensure that his community had access to firewood. The environmentalists agreed to sign off on two thinning areas in the Borrego Mesa area. The problem, he said, was that the Forest Service, particularly the Santa Fe National Forest, wasn't at the negotiating table as well; they were going to offer these thinning areas as commercial sales rather than local firewood sales. Ike explained that La Companía and the environmental groups that filed a lawsuit over La Manga had reached a potential settlement, but that the Forest Service would not release the sale, claiming the logging injunction imposed by the Arizona federal judge in the Mexican spotted owl lawsuit prevented them from doing so. La Companía planned to file a motion to find the Forest Service in contempt of court.

Everyone felt they needed to show their support of Truchas Land Grant members and Vallecitos loggers more directly. Glendinning pointed out that the Forest Service, like other bureaucracies, was being subsumed by corporate powers, and on-the-ground decisions continued to be made in Washington. It was agreed that the group needed to go public with their demands that the Forest Service respond to both the Truchas management plan (more on this later), written by the community, and the La Manga settlement, without further litigation.

A Stand Off

They indeed went public with their demands several weeks later on Halloween morning when norteños and their supporters, armed with chainsaws, headed out to Borrego Mesa on the Santa Fe National Forest, and prepared to cut firewood, illegally, if necessary, in a Forest Service thinning area set aside for commercial use. The day before, Max Córdova, along with Ike and Rio Arriba Green Party members, had arrived unannounced at the Española office of Lori Osterstock, District Ranger, with a letter stating that if the Forest Service didn't meet community members at La Joya de Arriba on Borrego Mesa and issue the firewood permits they claimed the Forest had initially promised them, they would harvest the wood without Forest Service permission.

The Forest Service arrived bright and early Thursday morning at the junction of the two forest roads that lead to the thinning areas, with a large, hand-lettered sign that read: "Firewood Permits Here." A timber staff technician was already at the thinning area, felling trees that were being sold as "dead and down" at $15 for two cords. At least five, armed, Forest Service law enforcement officers watched the proceedings (Max later told *La Jicarita* that he was offended by their presence).[33] Community members from Truchas, Chimayó, and Rio Chiquito immediately purchased permits and headed up the snow-covered road to the thinning area, in the Borrego burn area just before Borrego Mesa Campground. Ike, Max, Santiago Juarez, Sam Hitt of Forest Guardians, various Green Party members, and many reporters and photographers headed up with them, and those with chainsaws started bucking up the trees while everyone else helped load the trucks.

Ike sharpening his saw at the Borrego standoff

This thwarted confrontation was the result, according to Max, of Santa Fe National Forest's failure to offer 800 cords of wood that the grant deemed necessary to meet the firewood needs of the Truchas area (Truchas, Córdova, Cundiyó, Chimayó, Rio Chiquito). In the letter delivered to Osterstock, Max stated that on August 6 the Truchas Land Grant Commission met with Forest Service representatives and environmentalists Sam Hitt and John Talberth and everyone agreed that the two Borrego Mesa thinning areas, historically used by these communities, would be offered for fuelwood.

At the Borrego Mesa thinning area, Osterstock responded to the allegation that the Forest Service had reneged on its agreement with the communities and environmentalists by stating that the Forest

Service had previously offered fuelwood in a less accessible Borrego area, but when all the permits were not sold, and muddy roads forced a closure of the area, she assumed that there was no more demand for fuelwood. Max said that the sale Osterstock referred to was open for only two days, and advertised only in Truchas and Córdova.

Above and beyond the accusations made concerning the Borrego Mesa thinning area, valid concerns were being raised about the lack of local communities' involvement in forest decisions that affect them in very real and meaningful ways. In Max's letter to Osterstock, he also charged that the overall management plan of the Española District "is causing irreparable harm to our communities and our culture." He pointed out that the Forest Service was actually harvesting products from land patented to the Truchas Land Grant (Nuestra Señora del Rosario San Fernando y Santiago Land Grant) by the United States government. According to Max, when the United States Surveyor General surveyed the grant, he switched the described north and south boundaries of the grant, which resulted in the inclusion of Borrego Mesa within the grant boundaries. He accused the Forest Service of mismanagement of Borrego Mesa by employing clear cutting techniques rather than selective cutting and favoring commercial use over traditional use, which displaced and destroyed culture.

The Truchas Land Grant and the Forest Service negotiated a firewood management plan that could be implemented across the entire US Forest Service Region Three forest area. The grant asked that the plan include district advisory boards, implementation of the 1972 Region Three policy plan (the 1968 Hassell Report), and language that would explain the importance of firewood gathering to the communal traditions of northern New Mexico. Less dependency upon firewood as a fuel source (which was what Sam Hitt and other environmentalists continually promoted) was meaningless unless families had the money to install solar systems, add greenhouses, or buy natural gas. Once again, the powers that be forgot that activities like firewood gathering continued to connect people to the land. As Max pointed out, once that connection was lost, there would be less regard for and less stewardship of the land. "Reckless disregard" of community needs by the Forest Service or urban environmentalists, who favored litigation, would only result in further degradation of national resources. While this time Sam Hitt gave his support to the norteños, he acknowledged that there were serious differences between Forest Guardians and the loggers in the Vallecitos Federal Sustained Yield Unit, and that the La Manga lawsuit would, in all probability, only be resolved in court.

La Manga, Three Years Later

The Mexican spotted owl logging injunction was finally lifted in December 1996, but the La Manga lawsuit was still being negotiated. The Forest Service agreed to delay the award date of the sale to La Companía until the spring of 1997 so the logging company would not have to come up with sale money until they could access the unit (too much snow prohibited entry). An initial agreement would have had the Forest Service compensate La Companía for lost wages, due to the delay caused by the lawsuit, and provide a road-building credit, but then refused to do so unless the sale became a deficit sale.

The environmental groups agreed to try to raise $500,000 for a timber buyout; the money would be paid to La Companía in return for not logging the large diameter trees in the sale classified as old growth. Congressman Bill Richardson first proposed this compromise, whereby the Forest Service would have to come up with $100,000, the environmentalists between $200,000 and $300,000, and the balance from sources sought by the congressman. The Forest Service objected to the agreement, however, stating it was illegal to appropriate money to the loggers, even though the agency had agreed to compensate loggers in the Northwest to the tune of hundreds of millions of dollars.

While the McCune Foundation of Santa Fe was quoted as saying that this amount of money "was not out of reach," environmental groups had already filed a consistency lawsuit in Arizona, demanding that all forest activities be consistent with biological decisions made by the Forest Service. They included the La Manga timber sale in this lawsuit, despite the fact that Judge Mechem had declared that all decisions affecting the sale would be decided in his court. (Edwin Mechem was a well-respected judge who was also the judge in another extremely controversial case, the Aamodt Water Rights Adjudication, the longest-standing adjudication in New Mexico history.) John Talberth of Forest Guardians went on record saying his group was prepared to file hundreds of lawsuits over sales that they felt did not conform with revised Forest Service logging plans. After five large-diameter ponderosa pines were illegally cut in the La Manga sale unit in November, Sam Hitt called Ike an "environmental outlaw" and refused to ever negotiate with him again. This was in response to Ike's statement that while he was not responsible for the tree cutting, and he didn't encourage it, he was "sympathetic to it." Illegal tree cutting was a demonstration of the frustration and outrage local loggers felt at being out of work for such a long period of time.

Ike had always maintained that his company initially offered to negotiate the 500 acres of old growth contained in the sale if the environmentalists had agreed to release the remainder of the sale. Unless the environmentalists could come up with the $500,000 well before the release of the sale, they "won't have saved an owl or a tree." However, he also pointed out that if the 500 acres were included in the sale, "only one or two trees out of ten large trees per acre would be cut."

The new year, 1997, kicked off with more mediation sessions, labeled Roundtables, between environmentalists, the Forest Service, loggers, grazers, and their supporters. The press wasn't invited, but many people filled us in on the gist of the January meeting. According to Chellis Glendinning, the core group of environmentalists, who were involved in most of the litigious and controversial dealings with norteños, tended to dominate the meeting.

George Grossman of the Rio Grande Chapter of the Sierra Club, concurred with Glendinning. "My small group included Bill deBuys, the Forest Service District Ranger from Pecos, and Randy Schofield, a rancher from Tres Piedras, who voluntarily moved a good portion of his cattle off their grazing lands last year due to the drought. There wasn't much controversy anywhere except where Sam Hitt and John Talberth were. Sam kept talking about weatherizing homes in Truchas, which I didn't think was relevant to the discussion, and John kept talking about the sorry state of the forests in New Mexico, which I think is overstated. A percentage of the La Manga sale has been set aside as old growth, and we're only talking about an area of five percent where there are some big trees that will be cut. While I think Sam Hitt has been right about a lot of the issues over the years, I don't know why he's making such a fuss about these sales."[34]

In February of 1997 more than 80 people, including many well-known New Mexicans such as Lucy Lippard and Henry Carey of Forest Trust, signed a paid advertisement (drafted by Chellis Glendinning, myself, and a core group of activists) that appeared in two local papers, stating their support of the rights of indigenous peoples to "pursue the use of their traditional lands so that their unique cultures may survive." The signers made the distinction between wilderness that "should be left alone" and "inhabited wilderness, where people may live safely and sustainably," and perhaps most importantly, be sanctuaries against the encroachment of corporate globalization, an invaluable environmental strategy that everyone could support. In April of 1997, the Board of Directors of the Southwest Forest Alliance, a group of 55 conservation groups (of which Sam Hitt was a founding member), voted Hitt off the board. The board had met to set future policy, and apparently Hitt stormed out of the meeting after refusing to agree to the board's decision not to endorse a position calling for an end to all commercial logging on national forests ("Zero Cut" discussed in a following chapter). Hitt immediately sent out a press release stating that he had been ousted because of this disagreement. Board members, however, while acknowledging that they disagreed with Hitt on this policy, said he was kicked off the board because of his confrontational style and inability to get along with other members of the group. They also took him to task for his tendency to challenge too many Forest Service logging and controlled burn projects and his lack of commitment to local communities. Kieran Suckling, a board member and director of the Arizona-based Center for Biological Diversity, stated that Hitt's standing in the Southwestern environmental community began to slip in the fall of 1995 when he pushed for the restrictions on firewood gathering in northern New Mexico to protect the owl. Suckling said that most environmentalists didn't think the restrictions were necessary to protect the owl, but yielded to Hitt "because northern New Mexico was his backyard."[35]

Then, on May 5, US District Judge Edwin Mechem dismissed the La Manga timber sale lawsuit, filed almost three years earlier. La Companía de Ocho, would begin logging the first unit when the weather allowed; because of recent snow and rain, the area was too muddy to access. Loggers planned to harvest approximately one million board feet in the first unit, with a total sale volume of 2.1 million board feet. But the environmentalists went to the US Circuit Court of Appeals in San Francisco and filed an injunction against the sale. On June 27, in a separate ruling, US District Court in Phoenix stated that La Manga and 22 other timber sales in the Southwest did not have to conform to the latest Forest Service amended plans but only be consistent with the plans that were in existence at the time the sales were designed. The amended forest plans contained stricter logging restrictions for the protection of the Mexican spotted owl. In light of this ruling, the Forest Service and Rosenstock petitioned the San Francisco court to rescind the La Manga injunction for the sale to proceed. Forest Guardians appealed the Phoenix US District Court court ruling.

Inhabited Wilderness ad

PHOTO BY ERIC SHULTZ

Ike and John Talberth

As tensions heated up over the delays due to the ongoing legal actions, several protests were organized. On June 19, a protest in Santa Fe resulted in a shouting match between Ike and John Talberth of Forest Guardians (formerly of Forest Conservation Council). Then on June 23, a group of norteños walked into the Ghost Ranch conference grounds where Forest Guardians were holding a membership conference. They didn't disrupt the proceedings, but peacefully demonstrated against the "zero cut" policy being discussed, a policy of "no logging on public lands" that was being promulgated by environmentalists across the country.

Ike summed up his frustration. "The La Manga lawsuit was very debilitating for La Companía. We had to fight them in New Mexico Federal Court, Arizona Federal Court, and the Court of Appeals in San Francisco. We were shut out of the woods for almost three years because of that lawsuit and the spotted owl injunction and I had to go to work for Rio Arriba County. The environmentalists always find a pretext for their lawsuits. Here they were saying that La Manga should have been a restoration sale, but that's nonsense because they just appealed the Santa Fe Watershed, which is a restoration project. It's a pretext to block all forest management they don't approve of. They want only management by nature. They don't want any human intervention."

While the litigation dragged on La Companía bought the Jacques Tank sale and logged, milled, and sold it. They then got a loan from the bank to start work on La Manga. But between the time they won the suit in the New Mexico and Arizona federal courts and the San Francisco appellate court, Ike told me, "We did something that was probably forced on us in a sense, we went up and started cutting in La Manga even though the roads weren't completed. We needed to put the guys back to work and thought we needed to show the Court of Appeals that we already had timber on the ground and the roads were already started. That was a tactical thing we did that strategically was probably not a good thing. It also affected the negotiations about setting diameter limits for the timber we were cutting. We were prepared to go as low as 18 inches in diameter, but Sam Hitt of Forest Guardians was unwilling to negotiate, so that's why there is no diameter limit on pine. We were never given credit for being willing to compromise while they're given credit for being hardline."

PHOTO BY ERIC SHULTZ

Ike and Moises Morales at Ghost Ranch

La Compania Shut Down

When the lawsuits shut down La Compania's access to the woods Ike was hired to work for Rio Arriba County. "I started as risk manager. I did that for three years, and then when we won the suit against the environmentalists [over La Manga timber sale] I went back to work for La Compania and got it restarted. Then I went back to the county to work with the planning department after another lawsuit [Agua Caballos] shut La Compania down. I dealt with the county's timber harvest program. We got a timber harvest ordinance in place but I don't consider it a success because the county never adequately funded it. I found myself having to have timber harvest people transport me to the harvest areas for inspection because I didn't have the proper vehicle, particularly in the winter when there were 1,500 or 2,000 acres and you couldn't get through the snow to inspect it. I got discouraged working for the county because I felt it was passing ordinances in order to garner support from the voters without any intention whatever of enforcing them. Some people took the ordinances seriously and spent a lot of money to be in compliance. No reward for them. And for the people who ignored the ordinance, there was never any punishment. For example, after the county passed the agricultural ordinance to protect agricultural land from development, one of the commissioners subdivided 25 acres of irrigated land. These ordinances are selectively enforced and I'm very disappointed because for the most part they're good ordinances."[36]

Working at the county during the Democrats for Progress tenure (previously discussed) Ike tried to stay "outside" county politics where he saw that the patron system and nepotism were still extant. "It probably is pretty deeply ingrained in the culture because, let's face it, the largest employer in Rio Arriba County and probably all of northern New Mexico is government and local government in particular. Those who don't work for the schools, work for the county or for the city. Or Los Alamos [National Laboratory]. Los Alamos is a 900-pound gorilla in the whole picture. Other than that, there isn’t a whole lot of private industry providing jobs that have any kind of benefits like retirement and health insurance. . . So anyone is going to fight like crazy to keep his job. If that means electing someone who’s not going to make waves or ask too many questions and wants to play ball with the powers that be, well, they are going to do that. Yeah, they are using jobs to maintain political control. So it’s not important for them to hire the most qualified person. . . Whether it’s governing an acequia, governing a school, governing a county or city, well, it’s nepotism.”[37]

Chapter Four

Zero Cut

The "Zero Cut" logging initiative of Forest Guardians engendered both backlash and internecine conflicts within environmental groups that took a position on the issue. On June 4, 1997, a full-page ad appeared in *The New York Times* and the *Santa Fe New Mexican* entitled "Zero Cut Now." The ad, which called for a ban on all commercial logging on public lands (and solicited funds for Forest Guardians), was signed by a handful of national environmental groups including Earth Island Institute, the Constitution Law Foundation, Protect Our Public Lands, and Rethink Paper (a project of Earth Island Institute). Conspicuously absent was the Sierra Club, which a year before had passed a national referendum to end commercial logging on public lands.

Bruce Hamilton of the national Sierra Club conservation staff clarified why the Sierra Club hadn't signed the ad, saying there had been disagreement over the wording.[38] The Sierra Club decided that calling the ad "Zero Cut" would raise a red flag that might compromise the initiative's intent, which was to ban commercial industrialized logging on public lands. Using the words "Zero Cut" could give the wrong impression that the Club was opposed to cutting personal firewood or "cutting one's own Christmas tree." Hamilton said the Sierra Club would run its own ad in *The New York Times* to support Representative Cynthia McKinney's National Forest Protection and Restoration Act, introduced on October 31, 1997, which called for an end to commercial logging on all national forests and other federal public lands. The bill would leave intact firewood collection and "other traditional personal uses of the forest." It also called for a National Heritage Restoration Corps to restore federal forest lands to their natural condition and redirect logging subsidies to provide funds for worker retraining.

Hamilton admitted that even its own more carefully worded initiative had raised controversy within the rank and file of the Sierra Club. While Hamilton stated that members who disagree with the logging ban "should not be allowed to speak for the Sierra Club," the national organization authorized chapters to formulate their own forest management strategies based on local needs and politics.

PHOTO BY ERIC SHULTZ

Courtney White

The Santa Fe Group of the Sierra Club (later called the Northern Group) was one of the local groups that refused to support the ban. Courtney White, then chair of the Conservation Committee (and co-founder of the Quivira Coalition, an organization working with ranchers, farmers, government agencies, and land stewards to foster resilience on working lands), explicitly explained his reservations regarding the "Zero Cut" policy in his column in the Sierra Club publication *Rio Grande Sierran*, pointing out that if "we kill off rural communities" it is the developers, not "wildlife and other agents of biodiversity" that will step in to fill the vacuum. He chastised the membership that a no-logging policy is "elitist" and destroys the Club's ability to effect change and improvement of activities on public lands.[39]

As a result, David Orr, chair of the national Sierra Club No Logging Task Force, sent out a message on the Club's listserve attacking White and calling for his censure: "I call on the ExCom [Executive Committee] to take steps to bring the *Rio Grande Sierran* in line with national club policy. And I call on the ExCom to issue a formal apology in the next issue. This is an absolute disgrace, and all those who were elected to represent the members of the Rio Grande Chapter [parent of the Santa Fe Group] should be ashamed of yourselves. It's time to stop printing Wise Use rhetoric in Sierra Club publications."[40] ("Wise Use" refers to a movement founded by groups that support privatization and less government regulation under the guise of "stewardship").

Hamilton felt Orr had overstepped his bounds in calling for the censure of the Rio Grande Chapter of the Sierra Club, but reiterated that the national organization would continue to push for an end to all commercial logging, even if this policy failed to differentiate between corporate and small, locally based logging.

The Santa Fe Group found itself battling not only a national mandate but for its very survival. White lamented the Club's drift towards confrontation and no compromise on issues like commercial logging, and specifically pointed to Forest Guardians rising influence in the state chapter. "A determined effort by members, family, and friends of Forest Guardians to bend the Chapter to their 'take no prisoners' conservation philosophy is now underway."[41] Several Forest Guardian members held leadership positions in the "Zero Cut Campaign" (which later became the National Forest Protection Campaign) and ran for election to chair and executive committee positions in the Rio Grande Chapter of the Sierra Club. White went on to say how this was affecting the group as well. "Forest Guardians has been trying to strong-arm the Santa Fe Group of the Sierra Club for the last six months, demonstrating, through their actions, that they will not tolerate dialogue and collaboration. They certainly do not tolerate dissent."

PHOTO BY ERIC SHULTZ

Ike speaking at the Collaborative Stewardship conference in Taos

The issue that finally turned theoretical disagreement into all-out war was the Agua/Caballos timber sale in the Vallecitos Federal Sustained Yield. Remember, in 1995, La Companía was guaranteed 80 percent of the Agua/Caballos sale as settlement of their lawsuit against the Forest Service to comply with the terms of the Federal Sustained Yield Act. The Forest Service released the Agua/Caballos Draft Environmental Impact Statement (DEIS) in 1999, and the Santa Fe Group's Forest Issues Chair, George Grossman, submitted comments to the Forest Service supporting Preferred Alternative C, which called for a harvest of 10.6 million board feet in a 6,400-acre sale area. According to Grossman, the heavily overstocked sale area of the Unit could not only support this kind of a cut but was badly in need of it. In his letter Grossman acknowledged that while Sierra Club policy called for no commercial logging on public lands, at that time there was no legal mandate behind this policy and that it was impossible to manage the forests under current budget constraints without commercial logging. His comments were approved by the group's conservation chair, Cliff Larsen.

All hell broke loose two months later when Bryan Bird, the Conservation Biologist/Appeals Coordinator of Forest Guardians, who was also Secretary of the Rio Grande Chapter of the Sierra Club, filed a complaint stating that Grossman "violated club policy, misrepresented the Sierra Club, and misused the Sierra Club name and letterhead in an official capacity." He also stated that Grossman "should step down from his position with the Santa Fe Group and no longer volunteer his services to the Club."[42] Why he waited two months to file his complaint was unclear, but according to Santa Fe Group members, Bird submitted his letter to at least one national board member before he submitted it to the group, which contravenes Club procedure. Accusations among the group, chapter, and national levels started to fly once Bird's action became public, and the situation quickly degenerated into a Trial by Email, as several group members called it.

The implication of a "Trial" of George Grossman was offensive to many Club members and environmentalists familiar with Grossman's long and illustrious history. In particular, as Carson Forest Issues Chair for the Santa Fe Group, Grossman was intimately familiar with the entire forest, was actively involved in the creation of the Carson Forest Plan in the mid-1980s, and had successfully fought inappropriate timber sales like the Angostura on the Camino Real Ranger District. In fact, he was named a National Sierra Club Environmental Hero in 1992 for his work.

Ike and George Grossman at a La Jicarita party

The inherently hierarchical nature of the Club became apparent when the National Conservation Governance Committee issued a letter to members of the executive committees of the group and chapter requesting that a formal letter be sent to the Forest Service withdrawing the support of the Sierra Club for Alternative C, and that any further communication with the Forest Service or the press be made jointly from the group, the chapter, and the national. The group and chapter were given less than a week to address this request.

During this time of heightened tension between norteños and environmentalists, a group of activists had been meeting informally to support each other's work on issues of community forestry, water rights, land grant restitution, and economic justice: Chellis Glendinning, Ike DeVargas, Max Córdova, Eric Shultz, Mark and I were already immersed in forest and land grant politics while David Benavides and Pat D'Andrea primarily worked on water issues, David as a water rights attorney (with Northern New Mexico Legal Aid) and Pat as liaison between the environmental and social justice communities. Lisa Krooth, director of Legal Aid, provided agency support for La Companía's struggles to remain extant and for David's work for acequia communities. We invited George Grossman to participate in "El Grupo," as we humorously referred to ourselves, because of his battles within the Sierra Club over the "Zero Cut" policy and as a representative of the Santa Fe Group, whose members recognized that environmental issues do not exist in a social vacuum. Jake Kosek, doing his field work in Truchas for his PhD dissertation, was an honorary member (Kosek later wrote the definitive book about these contentious times: *Understories: The Political Life of Northern New Mexico Forests*).[43]

As pressure intensified on the Santa Fe Group, we decided upon a strategy to bring attention to the hierarchical nature of the Sierra Club and the absolutist policies—restricted immigration, "Zero Cut" and "Zero Cows" on public lands—that discriminate against and oppress rural and urban minorities. A few of us were already members of the Sierra Club; several more of us joined, and we decided to call a press conference to announce our resignation from the Club and the formation of our new organization, El Grupo. It was purely a publicity stunt, as none of us other than George were active members of the Club. While we'd already been meeting as El Grupo for quite a while, we figured it would help bring the debate before the public eye and shake up some folks in the Sierra Club.

We sent out a press release stating that the Sierra Club state chapter had placed a gag order on George and the Santa Fe Group, quoting Ike's response: "I am concerned about the heavy-handed tactics employed by the major environmental groups such as the Sierra Club to stifle dissent within their own rank, and by the vicious personal attacks employed when one of their members has the courage to say 'this is not right.'" The release went on to say that the mission of El Grupo would be "to work with community people and environmentalists to engage in meaningful dialogue and on-the-ground projects that develop rural livelihoods and provide good stewardship of the land. Members of the group will also speak out and condemn racist and elitist actions of groups such as Forest Guardians, Southwest Center for Biological Diversity, Audubon Society, The National Forest Protection Alliance, and the Wilderness Society, whose policies negatively impact the integrity of rural and urban communities."

On September 21 we held a press conference at the state capitol in Santa Fe. Moises Morales, former La Raza Unida Party member and then Rio Arriba County Commissioner, along with other local activists, came to support us. I read a statement detailing the controversy within the Club and our position; Ike read his own statement: "I am here today because major environmental organizations like the Sierra Club and the Sea Shepherds refuse to recognize the difference between a multi-national organization such as Duke City Lumber and a small local operation like La Companía de Ocho, or the major whaling companies and the Macah tribe in Washington, who only want to kill several whales per year in order to maintain their culture, customs, and traditions. The bigotry, elitism, and racism exhibited by these groups under the guise of environmental protection must be exposed so that the public can decide intelligently what the true state of the forest is, as opposed to the dishonest rhetoric spouted by the leadership of these organizations." We then took out our Sierra Club membership cards and tore them up (we'd debated whether to burn them, but this wasn't 1970).

The no-logging policy endorsed by the Sierra Club also elicited internal conflict and resignations in other major environmental organizations such as Earth Island Institute. Chellis Glendinning, who was then on the advisory board of Earth Island Institute, was

PHOTO BY ERIC SHULTZ

Press conference at the Capitol with Jake Kosek, Kay, Mark, Moises, Ike, and David Benavides

surprised when she saw that the Institute had signed onto the ad and immediately lodged a complaint with the organization. "I wrote to Earth Island and asked how it could take a public position—zero cut—that is insensitive to the basic questions of environmental justice," Glendinning said. "How could this organization, whose board of directors president is Carl Anthony, the African-American director of Urban Habitat, and whose board also includes people like Vandana Shiva, who has always worked for environmental justice, defend two conflicting policies?"[44] Others within the organization also expressed their disagreement with this public position, and an internal conflict with racial overtones erupted.

Chad Hanson, Co-Director (along win David Orr) of the John Muir Project, a project of Earth Island Institute, wrote a letter to Earth Island's board of directors, dated October 10, 1997, in which he stated that northern New Mexico was being deforested under the guise of environmental justice and that Carl Anthony, who traveled to New Mexico to meet with norteños, had been taken in by this "ruse" and had made racial attacks against Hanson and other people at Earth Island Institute. He also falsely accused Ike and other members of La Companía de Ocho of physically assaulting environmental activists. Hanson then went on at great length to assure the board that he was not a racist. "I don't have a racist bone in my body . . . Yet I have been the victim of racial prejudice by the President of Earth Island Institute . . . because I happen to have been born with a distinct lack of pigment in my skin."[45] Hanson, along with Emily Miggins of Rethink Paper, another Earth Island project, also wrote a letter claiming that Glendinning had a financial interest in La Companía and accused her of being a Wise Use member. These claims were patently untrue, of course, forcing Glendinning and Anthony, both social activists since the civil rights movement, to defend themselves.

In an attempt to address this conflict within Earth Island, a group of board members and advisors formed a committee to address the issue of environmental justice. In a mission statement presented to the board of directors they wrote: "Environmental justice is a philosophy and a practice that acknowledges both the ecological destruction wreaked upon the planet by mass technological societies and also the horrific social injustices—including racism, sexism, and economic inequities—that stem from the very same systems. In today's corporate global economy, the vanguard of environmentalism becomes not just the conservation of pure wilderness against the thrust of human civilization: it becomes the fostering of human survival through non-racist, non-sexist, economically equitable community living in direct and sustainable relationship to the Earth."

Chellis Glendinning, Ike, and Eric Shultz

Urban Habitat hosted a group of northern New Mexico community representatives and organized a demonstration at the November 6th hearings before the Ninth Circuit Court of Appeals in San Francisco, where Forest Guardians argued to further enjoin logging and grazing in US Forest Service Region Three. In a statement by Urban Habitat called "Fight the Corporate Destruction of Public Lands, Not Land-Based Communities," the group asked, "Why should we care about this struggle in New Mexico? Because decisions are being made here in the Bay Area without including the very people most affected." In January of 1998, a group of advisory and board members, including Anthony, as well as several projects, resigned from Earth Island Institute.

These kinds of conflicts and personal accusations towards Ike and activists like Chellis have real-life consequences. Chellis and Ike were good friends. They danced together when we all went to the Chamisa Inn in Española to hear Darren Córdova or Los Blue Ventures. Ike threw a party for her 50th birthday at his trailer in Servilleta Plaza (where he cooked outside because he had no stove and washed dishes in the river because he had no running water). She gave a fundraising party for him when he ran for Rio Arriba County sheriff on a "no more jails" platform (his campaign chest totaled enough for ten signs and one newspaper ad the day before the election). When accusations were made that Chellis had a financial interest in La Companía and Ike made so much money from logging that he owned two houses, we all had a good laugh. But these kinds of rumors can have grave consequences in worlds where people lack information and relationship: Chellis subsequently resigned from Earth Island Institute's board of advisors when the organization failed to respond to Urban Habitat's protest, and she eventually broke relations with other people in the national environmental community who saw her support of the Vallecitos loggers as a betrayal of her commitment.

Ike and Chellis Glendinning

La Manga Released

In September of 1997 the Ninth Circuit Court of Appeals in San Francisco denied the environmentalists' last emergency motion to stop the La Manga timber sale. On a warm, fall afternoon Ike went out to the sale and felled some of the ponderosa pines that had become a symbol of everything wrong in a movement that had alienated both Indigenous communities and its own community as well. Sam Hitt said to reporters, “We lost. We've been failed by politics to protect the public interest.” The public interest that Hitt always said he was protecting was the interest of urban environmentalists whose sense of what constitutes environmental health and biodiversity was based on the wilderness ethic of “visitor only.” The concept of “inhabited wilderness” was alien to their experience as weekend recreationists and how they perceived the deep ecology ethic that separates people from the natural landscape. After La Manga was released, several environmentalists from Forest Trust, a non-profit forestry consultant based in Santa Fe that community-based foresters and activists had worked with on many issues in the Carson and Santa Fe forests, toured the sale and observed, “La Manga is a good prescription.”

Ike continued to be hopeful that future meetings with environmentalists would prove fruitful, that together they could sit down and actually write timber sale plans that the Forest Service would implement and professional environmentalists would recognize as both protective of communities and resources. After so many meetings, group affiliations, alliances, and subsequent breakdowns, it was remarkable that Ike maintained a faith in people and a faith in the process.

On Tuesday, September 30, La Companía began cutting the first unit of the La Manga timber sale. This is what Ike had to say to the public:

“I don't see that the fight is over yet. But we need to leave some of the animosity behind and learn from this experience. The main thing we need to do is educate the people, especially the new people who are coming into our area, on how we can sustainably live the way we traditionally have. I don't know how easy it's going to be to heal the wounds that were created by this fight. There's a lot of anger out there. One of the ways we can go about this is by meeting with open-minded environmentalists and open-minded users of the land; ranchers, loggers, and wood haulers, and try to get a sane, unified voice out there. Things are so polarized now that we can't do anything. We must try not to be so confrontational, if we can.

"What I suggest we do is get core groups of open-minded people to go out to the sales like Agua/Caballos before they are released, maybe next spring, and see what the on-the-ground conditions are and talk about what we're going to do, using La Manga as a comparison. I think the prescriptions that I've seen in La Manga are pretty good. The forest needs to stay healthy and have big trees. There are some beautiful stands of ponderosa in the Agua/Caballos, but some of them are overgrown, too. We need to see what kind of prescriptions might be helpful in there without destroying the old growth or the potential old growth. I still believe that there are some old growth stands that need to be thinned out because of their high mortality rate. But in most cases there are also, right there, what we call potential old growth stands that shouldn't be touched. In that way you always have old growth. If the Forest Service had been managing this way we wouldn't be having all these hassles. We always told the foresters that in the Sustained Yield Unit we don't want a tree farm. We want an uneven-aged forest. Also, these forests should support the animals that are there, not the animals that aren't there. If historically there has not been an endangered species there, then why try to manage for something that's not there.

"I also think people should start looking at how the forests can be managed, through logging and thinning practices, for the production of water quantity and higher quality water. Because that can be done. We need to start sharing this information with all the communities in northern New Mexico. Many people instinctively know what is good or bad for the forests, but they don't have all the scientific data they need to better manage the forests. We had a meeting with the regional and district Forest Service managers and we told them that they need to make this data more available, if not directly to the communities at least to their elected officials: county commissioners, city councilors, mayors, etc. This is an educational process. People who haven't spent a lot of time in the forest or made a living off the forest often have a knee-jerk reaction to the word logging or cattle grazing. There will, unfortunately, continue to be confrontation because some of these environmentalists refuse to admit that they were wrong. I know that Forest Guardians doesn't think there was any social or political problem with what happened in the last nine years. So there may be people like that who we can never reach. But we have to reach the other people, newcomers especially."[46]

The Bomb

After the release of the La Manga timber sale, Sam Hitt and other environmentalists continued their attacks, which often included *La Jicarita News*'s coverage of their appeals and lawsuits against Ike and La Companía. It reached its nadir in 1999. On March 19, a pipe bomb was found in the mailbox of Forest Guardians in Santa Fe. Fortunately, the bomb failed to go off, but several days later the group received an envelope in the mail with a drawing of a rifle scope's cross hairs over the words "Forest Guardians" and "see-ya" written underneath. It was signed "MM—The Minute Men."

On March 23, Charlotte Talberth, former Forest Guardians board member and wife of Forest Conservation Council co-founder John Talberth, sent the following e-mail to a person or persons unknown:

"Today at 10:15 am Forest Guardians' chief canvasser, Mike Cherin, discovered a pipe bomb when he opened the mailbox outside Forest Guardians' office in Santa Fe. The bomb did not explode and no one was hurt. Police bomb squads subsequently arrived and detonated the bomb, which was loaded with ball bearings, meaning it was designed to kill.

Last week Rio Arriba County hosted a day-long meeting of officials from counties in Northern New Mexico and Southern Colorado. The purpose of the meeting was to get more counties to join Rio Arriba in intervening against Forest Guardians et al. in the national economic lawsuit, and to censure the State of the Southern Rockies report authored by John Talberth and Bryan Bird [a Wildlands report].

The people who spoke at the meeting are all known to us—Ike deVargas [sic], Santiago Juarez, Chellis Glendinning and Richard Rosenstock. They foment hatred and violence against Forest Guardians and Zero Cut on a regular basis by calling us genocidal racists etc. in public forums and publications, particularly *La Jicarita*, a newsletter circulated in Northern New Mexico. According to Bryan Bird, who was there, numerous threats of violence were made at the meeting. We are very, very thankful that Mike was not killed. I can post whatever stories are printed in tomorrow's papers. Mike says it makes him want to work harder than ever."

Andy Caffrey of the Earth First! Media Center somehow received the e-mail and immediately sent it to a "Recipient List Suppressed." All of us who "foment hatred and violence" soon saw a copy of it. Talberth attempted to do damage control with a subsequent e-mail to Andy Caffrey stating, "had I known that that email was going to be forwarded to you and then broadcast, I would have been clearer in stating that I have no reason to believe that any particular individuals were directly involved in the attack. It was never my intention to add to the already divisive dynamic that exists between people who should by rights be allies: those who claim to speak for local rural people and those who claim to speak for the environment."

Those of us named in Talberth's email met several times at Richard Rosenstock's office, with fellow civil rights attorney Bob Rothstein, to discuss whether we should file a defamation lawsuit against her. After a lot of venting and back and forth, we decided against it, as it wouldn't help our cause much in the long run. She was already in retreat.

No one was ever arrested for placing the pipe bomb in Forest Guardians' mailbox.

Chapter Five

Agua/Caballos Timber Sale

The Agua/Caballos timber sale in the Vallecitos Federal Sustained Yield Unit was long in the making: public involvement began in 1992; two Draft Environmental Impact Statements (DEIS) were released, in 1995 and 1999; a supplement to the DEIS was issued in 1999; and many public meetings and field trips were held over the course of the project. The second DEIS was released to comply with the amended Carson Forest Plan, and the supplement to the 1999 DEIS was issued in response to discrepancies regarding the actual number of road miles needed to implement the Preferred Alternative. Two new alternatives were included in the supplement that prohibited any new road building, and an Alternative G was developed that minimized road building while still meeting the purpose and need of the proposal and became the Preferred Alternative.

The public participation was vast. Two Vallecitos teenagers, Lucas Culin and Gabe Aldaz, spent several months producing overlay maps of the proposed sale, coordinated by Forest Trust. The maps provided information on existing old growth, roads, timber types, perennial and intermittent streams, Mexican spotted owl habitat, semi-primitive designation, and previous timber sales.

Community members attended a field trip to the Agua/Caballos area on Friday, June 11, 1999 and used these maps to get an overview of the sale before walking specific areas to look at on-the-ground conditions. Representatives from Madera Forest Products, La Companía de Ocho (including Ike, of course), the Santa Fe Group of the Sierra Club, Forest Trust, the Audubon Society, the Rio Pueblo/Rio Embudo Watershed Protection Coalition, and several other individuals attended the tour to educate themselves and to demonstrate that they were interested in promoting a good sale prescription that provided for forest health and met the economic and personal firewood needs of the surrounding local communities. The Forest Service was not invited on this tour, though the group was working with El Rito District Ranger Kurt Winchester, who succeeded Graciela Terraza and had expressed his willingness and enthusiasm to meet and discuss the sale with the group.

Chellis, Ike, Henry Carey of Forest Trust, George Grossman

The Agua/Caballos analysis covered a large area—23,767 acres—and the Forest Service preferred alternative proposed a substantial timber cut, including fuelwood, thinning, and sawtimber. But the sale would actually take place over a period of years in smaller sale units in a 6,400-acre area. Both the Forest Service and many of those who participated in the June tour believed that the proposed harvest was sustainable and necessary to treat the overstocked and unhealthy conditions of much of the sale area. La Companía, which still had 1.5 million board feet of timber to harvest in La Manga timber sale, would probably harvest less than a million board feet per year over a number of years in Agua/Caballos. The Forest Service, however, was anxious to release the sale after five years of planning, to provide for community fuelwood.

With the release of the Agua/Caballos timer sale, La Companía and Madera Forest Products could have potentially joined forces (they are comprised of many of the same people) to keep 50 community people working in the VFSYU. They needed adequate equipment, however, including a larger capacity saw (remember, the Vallecitos sawmill, formerly owned by Duke City Lumber, was donated to another community group, Las Comunidades, but needed to be refurbished before it could be used) and a kiln drier, as well as an administrative staff that could handle marketing, planning, and Forest Service liaison. Hopefully, this would be the next step in a progression of positive things that had happened in the previous few years in the VFSYU: community groups organizing and fighting for self-determination and economic parity; Duke City finally releasing its stranglehold and resigning as the approved operator; and the Forest Service changing its policies concerning both meeting national guidelines for forest health and endangered species requirements as well as the needs of the local communities. Those who participated in the tour wanted to support these efforts and ensure that this sale would continue to protect and promote these past achievements of forest and community sustainability.

The Forest Service released the Record of Decision and Final Environmental Impact Statement (FEIS) for the Agua/Caballos Proposed Projects on June 3, 2002. It was appealed in August by Joanie Berde of Carson Forest Watch, Paul Becker of Vallecitos Stables, John Horning of Forest Guardians, and Sam Hitt of Wild Watershed (Hitt had left Forest Guardians to found Wild

Watershed that focused on the Santa Fe watershed several years earlier). Under National Environmental Policy Act (NEPA) regulations, Wild Watershed didn't have standing to appeal and was dismissed from the process.

The appeal accused the Forest Service of failing to gather the necessary. population data for indicator species in the VFSYU as required by the National Forest Management Act (NFMA). The appeal claimed that the agency relied on "habitat trend data" instead of acquiring the population data it needed to provide for the diversity of plant and animal communities in the area. Kurt Winchester, who was then acting as assistant Carson National Forest Supervisor, met with both Berde and Becker in an effort to negotiate a settlement to their appeal (Forest Guardians was also invited but declined to participate). According to Winchester, the discussion with the two appellants focused more on their desire that no trees over 18 inches be harvested rather than the issues raised in the appeal. "I'm disappointed that this appeal is all about process rather than the merits of our decision. An appeal like this subverts the efforts of the many people and organizations who contributed to the modification of the original proposal, including Paul Becker, whose comments were specifically addressed in the FEIS [Final Environmental Impact Statement]. I'm confident that the decision will be upheld."[47]

George Grossman, as Carson National Forest timber coordinator for the Santa Fe Group of the Sierra Club, had both organized and attended many field trips to the site and as I referenced previously, had commented on all the draft versions of the sale, despite the national Sierra Club's opposition to commercial timbering on public lands. According to Grossman, "The Sustained Yield Unit is something very special, an area set aside by the federal government to economically benefit the local communities, and as such it should get special consideration." He pointed out that before the area was in the public domain, it was heavily logged, with many clearcuts: "As long as the

Forest Service is committed to setting aside the required 20 percent old growth, I'm not concerned that the prescription includes some big trees," Grossman said.[48]

Because the designated operators within the VFSYU were relatively small businesses, it was likely that only 500,000 to one million board feet a year would be cut in the project. Winchester pointed out, however, that if the operators coordinated their efforts and pooled their resources they could potentially harvest between one and two million board feet a year.

In response to the appeal of the Record of Decision in 2002, Carson National Forest released a Supplement to the Final Environmental Impact Statement (FEIS) for the Agua/Caballos Proposed Projects in the summer of 2003. The appeal was upheld by the Deputy Regional Forester, who directed the Carson to "complete the analysis of effects on management indicator species (MIS) considering population and habitat information collected at the forest plan level or at an appropriate geographical scale for a particular species." This analysis was included in the Supplemental FEIS; Alternative G remained the preferred alternative.

Otra vez, a year later, the same environmental groups appealed the Supplemental FEIS. Felipe Martinez, of Las Comunidades, one of the designated operators, had been slowly building capacity with the help of United States Department of Agriculture (USDA) grants that were used to purchase equipment and develop a business plan. He pointed out that even if his company was unable to bid on sawtimber it could bid on the fuelwood, vigas, latillas, and cedar post sales. Martinez went on to say that Las Comunidades had been working hard to raise awareness of the importance of the Vallecitos Federal Sustained Yield Unit. "The Unit was all former grant lands that sustained the people of the villages of Vallecitos, Cañon Plaza, Servilleta, and Petaca. The environmentalists in Santa Fe just don't get it; these communities have been forest-based for hundreds of years. Horning [John Horning of

Forest Guardians] thinks the people need to leave the communities and get other jobs. So where are these jobs? In Española, where the people already there can't find work? In the meantime, they don't care that community-based businesses become insolvent."[49]

In an even more sober assessment of the fallout from the controversial history of Agua/Caballos, Ike, who had already quit La Companía de Ocho, said, "The Forest Service and the environmentalists have succeeded in getting the people of the Sustained Yield Unit villages fighting each other. And until we find a unity of purpose, we will have nada. We're a community divided, beating each other up for the crumbs."[50]

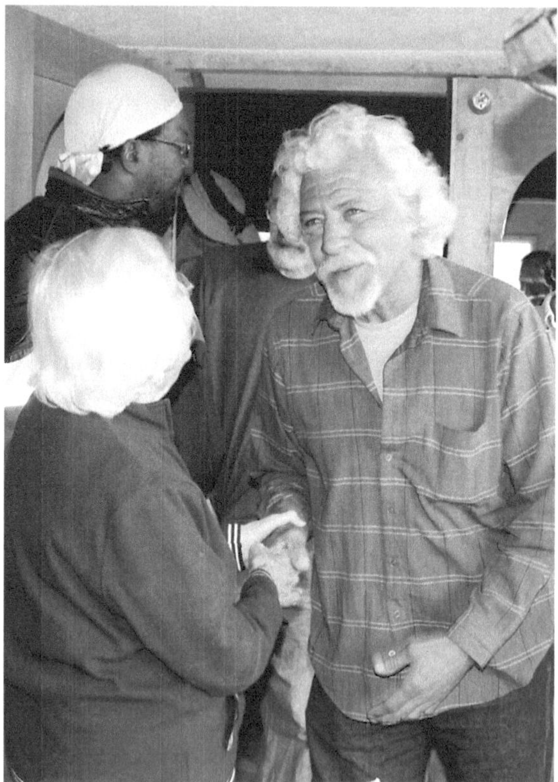

Ike in El Valle

The appeal was denied, and thirteen years after its conception, in May of 2005, Forest Guardians and Carson Forest Watch took the ultimate step of filing a lawsuit to stop the sale from moving forward. After two Draft Environmental Impact Statements, years of public comment, numerous field trips to the site, two Final Environmental Impact Statements, two appeals, and the demise of any designated operators with the capacity to harvest the sale, the lawsuit was simply beating a dead horse.

Bryan Bird of Forest Guardians and Joanie Berde of Carson Forest Watch were both quoted in the *Taos News,* making it clear that the lawsuit was about cutting big trees: Bird called the sale "old school" and Berde said "cutting old growth trees is pretty senseless these days." After 20 years of appealing and litigating timber sales, these groups helped kill community-based forestry in the VFYSU. According to Ike, "There's no capacity to log in the Unit. None of the designated operators can handle a sale like Agua/Caballos. La Companía filed for bankruptcy and sold off its equipment. Everyone keeps saying that [President George W.] Bush is in there tearing up the forest, but it's not happening in the Unit. Nothing is getting cut."[51] El Rito District Ranger Diana Trujillo, who succeeded Kurt Winchester, was encouraging small loggers still working in the Unit to collaborate on projects, but it was unlikely that the few remaining designated operators had the capacity to bid on the 6.3 mmbf Agua/Caballos sale.

Ike went on. "I still think conditions exist, from the work that La Companía and Las Comunidades have done, for a local logging group to get together to successfully finish the sales in the Unit. They could take advantage of the performance bonds and the roads we've already built, and that would be a big leg up. I'd like to see it happen. But one of the biggest obstacles is getting the financing from the banks. Another gripe I have about Bill Richardson is that when he was our representative he could have put some teeth in the Community Reinvestment Act to support small, rural businesses like it was supposed to. We could have gotten bank loans at seven percent rather than at the 10.75 we had to pay. We also could have probably gotten a longer payout period. As it was, we were paying quarterly payments on a $250,000 loan and consequently we were always paying on the interest and never made any headway on the principal. I think the Community Reinvestment Act could support northern New Mexico entrepreneurs with a good payout that would really help us get a step up.

"I think that everyone pretty much got burned out, and I don't blame them because it takes a lot of energy. And I don't have the energy either. I intend to still go to the woods to rejuvenate my body and my spirit, to fish and hike and camp. I don't want people to think that we were just a bunch of mean-spirited people who went out to the woods to cut old growth and to let them rot in the woods just to bug Sam Hitt and the environmental community. That's not what this was about. People need to know why it happened."

Ike, campfire cook

Chapter Six

Ike Takes on Rio Arriba County—Again

In October, 2001, a month after the September 11 attacks on New York's World Trade Center and the Pentagon, *La Jicarita* interviewed Ike about his response. He had quit both La Companía and Rio Arriba County for health reasons and because he was just damned tired.

La Jicarita News: As a northern New Mexico community activist and Vietnam veteran, what's your perspective on what's going on in the Middle East and Afghanistan?

DeVargas: The Palestinian people are not that different than the Spanish-speaking people and Native American people in New Mexico. We both had our lands stolen and have been politically disenfranchised. The world powers set up Israel to dispossess the Palestinian people just like they stole the land grants here. The only difference is that we're much richer here and our situation isn't as desperate as that in the Middle East. Really, rural people everywhere in the world suffer under these same conditions. Look at what's happening to the farmers in the Klamath Valley in Washington. The government ends up creating these terrorist groups with their arrogance and oppression. I'm fearful that if this situation escalates into a real war young, rural, Hispano men will become cannon fodder while the old people will be left to try to take care of things. This will lead to more dispossession of the land.

La Jicarita News: How would you gauge the reaction of the people of northern New Mexico to the attacks?

DeVargas: Many people are not questioning the government line regarding the situation out of fear, but I see other people calling for restraint and asking questions about why this happened. I'm part of the grassroots. People here are very stoic; they have to deal with life on a day-to-day basis. Unless things hit them with a double-barreled shotgun they don't react. While my colleagues in Rio Arriba County are fully aware of the situation, they have no sense of panic or dread. They do worry, however, that there will be cutbacks in county services as money gets directed towards national defense. You already read about environmental groups taking a softer approach to the Bush administration, saying we have to support our president in this crisis. But I think we need to be very vocal in our support of social programs and not let the government siphon all the money towards an anti-terrorist campaign.

La Jicarita News: You mentioned that you are fearful that there will be more terrorism in this country because of our government's arrogance. Can you talk about this some more?

DeVargas: We're already seeing it happen. Timothy McVeigh wasn't from the Middle East. The militia groups are becoming potential terrorist groups. There are millions of oppressed people in this country. For example, the Bureau of Indian Affairs mismanaged at least $10 billion in trust fund money belonging to Native American tribes. These people need that money desperately for economic development and tribal infrastructure, but do you think they're ever going to see it now? The same thing is happening to the Mexican and South American immigrants. We take advantage of their cheap labor and then direct our hostility at them. In this country the poor are getting poorer and the rich are getting richer. We're developing a caste system where soon there will be no middle class. Money is the only measure of success in this country.

La Jicarita News: In previous conversations you've talked about how you were politicized by your experiences in Vietnam. Is there more dissent about government policy in New Mexico because of our history of colonization?

DeVargas: I volunteered for a Special Forces unit in Vietnam, the same kind of unit they're now sending into Afghanistan. But I realized by observing and interacting with the rural people in Vietnam that we shared the same history as colonized people. I think the Hispano people in New Mexico have slowly been politicized. The United States government has not honored the Treaty of Guadalupe Hidalgo and many ask why they should defend the country that has stolen their land. By and large we're good people, but as a society, our eyes are closed. Now is the time to ask why we're so hated. Most of the people who attended a town meeting with Representative Tom Udall last week in Santa Fe asked this question and expressed their desire that we not respond with violence. I think there's a lot of frustration with the political establishment. The worst enemy of a free society is the power elite, represented in this country by congress and corporations. We all know that money buys political office and there's no grassroots representation. The media, newspapers, and television are complicit with these government and corporate interests. Masked under the face of compassion they raise money for the victims of the attacks that buys support for their oppressive policies.

La Jicarita News: How have these policies affected your logging company, La Companía de Ocho?

DeVargas: As a veteran I qualify for low interest veteran loans, but there's not a bank in Rio Arriba County that will support a VA [Veterans Administration] loan. I've never gotten a loan, homeowner or business, below a 10 percent interest rate. And I know why—the banks don't want to carry a lower rate than what they can conventionally get. They take it for granted that the poor are powerless and can't effectively complain about it. A lot of us don't live any differently than our parents did during the Depression. I still live without running water. The odds are stacked against minority small business people. This may be the end of La Companía. Foundations underwrite non-profits but are reluctant to fund for-profits. It's ironic in a capitalistic society that we even have to consider going to them. But the market economy works against us. Our overhead is prohibitive because of the insurance costs we have to carry as subcontractors who work for larger companies that don't have to cover us.

***La Jicarita News*:** What advice would you give your community about how we should proceed.

DeVargas: I hope clearer minds will prevail. We need to look in our own backyards for the terror we create here. We can bring terrorists to justice without invading countries. But we need to ask ourselves, is this terrorism or guerrilla action? Oppressed people can be inspired to raise hell. It's the easiest thing in the world for four or five people who feel they are in desperate situations to be willing to give their lives in various guerrilla activities. We're letting other countries like Israel dirty their hands for us. A lot of the so-called terrorists have been trained by the CIA or the School of the Americas to fight to protect our interests. Now they're using that training and weaponry, which we've supplied, to protect their own interests. We've created our own demons. I hope people open up their eyes. We're already involved in a civil war in our own society. Look at all the murders. Look at the drug use. Look at the number of people in jail for nonviolent crimes. People are turning their anger inward. Level-headed Americans need to speak out.

......

As Ike predicted, by 2006 commercial logging in the Vallecitos Federal Sustained Yield Unit was dead. Instead, under a program initiated by former New Mexico Senator Jeff Bingaman in 2000, a Forest Service program called the Collaborative Forest Restoration Program (CFRP) provided $5 million a year to US Forest Service Region Three for small, timber-related projects that focused on thinning and prescribed burning in the overstocked and unhealthy forests of northern

New Mexico. *La Jicarita* wrote a critique of the program in the July, 2004 issue that analyzed its effectiveness and fairness. According to the Forest Service, as of March 2004, with grants of $11.8 million dispersed, a total of 3,992 acres had been treated (95 percent of grantees reporting), with a projected total acreage of 11,126. Acres treated included 1,805 of mixed conifer/ponderosa pine, 1,398 of piñon pine/juniper, and 789 of bosque. Many community foresters believed this limited amount of acreage was due to the fundamental problems inherent in the program.

One such problem was apparent on the El Rito Ranger District in 2006. In a *La Jicarita* article titled "Environmental Politics in Northern New Mexico: "Revisionist Spin Suggests 'It's All Good,'" Mark and I wrote an editorial about an article published in *High Country News* in which Forest Guardians, the Collaborative Forest Restoration Program director, former Madera Forest Products director Luis Torres (who was on the *High Country News* board of directors), and logger Alfonso Chacon claimed that the logging economy in New Mexico has been "brought back to life" and "peace has broken out in our forests." In our editorial we wrote, "On the one hand, everything is hunky dory because Forest Guardians is working with community forester Alfonso Chacon on a 260-acre thinning project in the Vallecitos area with the help of a CFRP grant, while on the other hand, after spending $25 million, less than 20,000 of 3.3 million acres of overgrown forests have been treated and many community foresters have been put out of business because of environmental lawsuits and Forest Service mismanagement. But hey, nobody's been hung in effigy lately, so it's all good, que no?" The author of the article never interviewed Ike or Max Córdova or any of the other loggers who lost their jobs and livelihoods due to Forest Guardian lawsuits and Forest Service mismanagement.

It's not in the purview of this book to discuss the evolution of the CFRP program, which essentially became the only game in town as

Forest Service funding was repeatedly slashed throughout the 2000s. The agency became increasingly dependent on programs such as the CFRP and other innovative attempts to put the people of northern New Mexico—individuals and small contractors—to work on Wildland Urban Interface, fuelwood, and watershed restoration projects. Ike's work in the woods was done. But his political work wasn't—and never would be.

In 1997, when Third Congressional District Representative Bill Richardson quit his Democratic seat to be the United Nations Ambassador under President Bill Clinton, a special election was held to replace him. The Democrats picked Eric Serna of Española, who served on the Public Regulation Commission and was later accused of intervening in an automobile accident insurance claim involving his daughter. The Republicans picked Los Alamos minister Bill Redmond, and the Greens, who had drawn ten percent of the vote in the 1994 gubernatorial race, nominated health activist Carol Miller of Ojo Sarco. Serna was a holdover pick from the Emilio Naranjo era, supported by mainstream Democratic Party insiders, and Ike threatened to run against him as an Independent. Redmond won with 43 percent of the vote (Carol Miller got 17 percent). He lasted only one term.

PHOTO BY ERIC SHULTZ

Ike and Max at Chellis Glendinning's campaign party

Around the same time, Ike actually ran for Rio Arriba County Sheriff on a platform of "No more jails." Max Córdova ran for the Rio Arriba County Commission at the same time. Neither was elected.

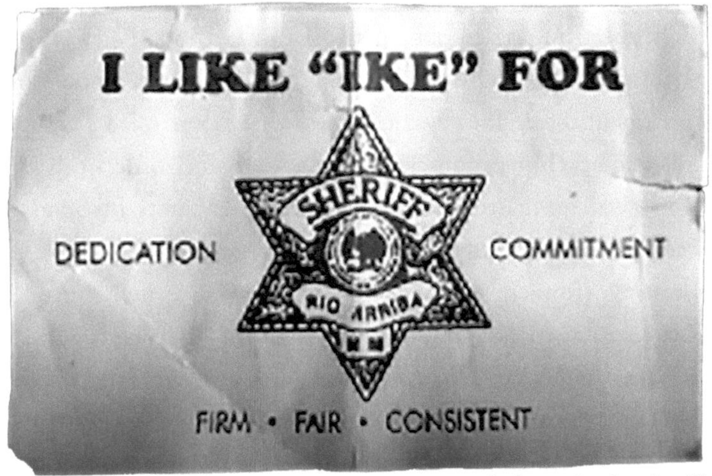

Ike's poster for sheriff

PHOTO BY ERIC SHULTZ

Max Schiller, Kay Matthews, Ike, Richard, Moises at Chellis' campaign party

Ironically, many years later, in 2010, Wilfred Romero ran for Rio Arriba County Sheriff along with five other dubious characters. Romero was an associate warden at the New Mexico Penitentiary when Ike was held there for safekeeping by the Rio Arriba County District Attorney in 1976 after he beat up the off-duty sheriff's deputy outside the Chamisa Inn, as described in the La Raza Unida Party chapter. Ike named Romero in his 1977 lawsuit against the Penitentiary over his treatment there. The lawsuit claimed that Romero led a group of guards who beat him unconscious and then left him in a dark cell without food, water, a mattress, or a toilet for four days until his bond was posted. Romero claimed he wasn't a supervisor then and didn't lead the beating. (Romero was named as a defendant as Superintendent nine times in district court lawsuits and 18 times in federal court lawsuits.) In a May 13, 2010 *Rio Grande Sun* article, Ike had this to say: "I still consider the son of a (expletive) an animal. He and 10 other guards beat me to within an inch of my life. He brutalized a hell of a lot of inmates, and now just the other day I heard he's running for sheriff. That's just not right."

North Central Waste Management Authority

Ike's troubles with Rio Arriba County resurfaced around 2006 when the county's trash contractor, North Central Solid Waste Authority, claimed he hadn't paid his trash bill—he had—put a lien on his property, and never allowed him a hearing on the lien, which is required by Rio Arriba County Ordinance 97-04 that established the Authority. Thus began his long look into Authority practices that revealed misappropriated public money, billed and collected money for services not rendered, and other illegal acts.

When Ike first saw the "Public Notice" flier the Authority had sent out to customers, numerous red flags were raised. The flier stated that all county residents are "Mandated" (in quotes, bold, and underlined) to pay the solid waste fees, not for "service" but "for the solid waste system in place." It went on to say that the ordinance establishing the Authority authorizes it to "assign an account for any *habitable* dwelling" within the county (added emphasis). Finally, it states that a signature is not required to execute a valid agreement.

The Authority's mandate to require residents to pay solid waste fees whether they actually utilize the system, or even sign for it, has resulted in a long list, which Ike acquired, of hundreds of residents with delinquent accounts: because there is no "habitable" dwelling on the property, the inhabitant is not living on the property and therefore not generating trash, or the inhabitant is dead. Once these delinquent accounts accrue, a lien is placed on the property, with a four-year limit (although penalties and taxes can still accrue). The liens state that the payment is for "pickup, transport, and treatment," none of which applies when there is no generated trash. Ike emphasized that a lien should be on an inhabitant, not the land. "The land lives forever and doesn't produce trash."

Residents pay a yearly fee of $230 to the Authority. From 2008 to 2012 Rio Arriba County paid a $4 million subsidy to the Authority, essentially a double tax on county residents for a "system" many of them don't use. In 2013 the Authority amended its bylaws to address this issue of exemptions, such as seasonal homes and vacant land, and redefined "habitable" to mean a home with electricity. Any home, whether it generates trash or not, is considered habitable if it has power. The then Authority manager Gino Romero admitted that establishing what houses qualify for exemptions was an arduous process, which was made very clear by the long lists of delinquencies (over 1,000) Ike provided that revealed uninhabited properties and dead people. (Under current "leadership," "P[p]oor accounting, lack of checks and balances, missing documents and an inability to balance ledgers" was rampant, according to the *Rio Grande Sun*.[52] The former Authority manager, Joseph Lewandowski, left his job in 2009 with the Authority $2.3 million in debt.)

In 2019 Ike and Donald Orie, both of whom had liens put on their properties, collected 527 signatures on a petition calling for a grand jury investigation of the Authority. The petition alleged the Authority committed "malfeasance, misappropriated public money, billed and collected money for services not rendered, and committed other non-specified illegal acts." The petition was filed in First Judicial District Court, and on November 8, Judge Jason Linyard announced he would convene a special grand jury (a sitting grand jury would not have sufficient time) to investigate the allegations. The judge predicted the jury would be empaneled by February of 2020, but the case was put on hold due to the outbreak of the coronavirus.

Ike in El Valle

Ike wanted the county to discard the liens and then repeal Rio Arriba County Ordinance 97-04 and start from scratch with community input. He suggested that the county implement a fee-for-service system whereby residents could pay a flat fee to bring trash to a transfer station. Currently, those who qualify for self-haul (those who live on roads that the Authority trucks are too big to access or in distant areas where the county can't provide curb-side pick-up) take their trash to the existing transfer stations (in Española, Truchas, and Alcalde) for about half the fee of curb-side pickup. They're provided with punch cards to regulate the amount of trash they can deposit.

At a 2021 Rio Arriba County Commission meeting Ike shared stories of local Española businesses that have trash accounts with MCT Waste, LLC, a statewide service, which provides better service for less money. These businesses are still required to pay Authority fees. Ike told the commissioners, "The Authority is a monopoly, extorting its customers." Peter Romero, who attended Ike's presentation, told his sad story of discovering a lien had been placed on property he hadn't resided on for years because of a medical condition. He'd been staying with his son in Phoenix so he could attend the Mayo Clinic, and when he tried to get a mortgage on a different property he owned to pay for a liver transplant, he was denied because of the lien. He had to hire attorney Richard Rosenstock to negotiate with the Authority and release him from the lien.

The response from the county commissioners was a mixture of "we hear your pain" and "I wasn't on the commission when the ordinance was passed," except, of course, for Moises Morales, who was on that commission. Commission Chairman James Martinez pointed out that the county didn't run or dictate the Authority and was only a party to the Joint Powers Agreement signed by the city, county, and pueblos (Ohkay Owingeh and Santa Clara). Ike believed that because the county created the Authority it could repeal the Ordinance. Martinez, who also served on the Authority's Board of Directors, along with county manager Lucia Sanchez, said that the board was getting new members and reviewing policies, operations, and payments. Manager Sanchez stated that the Authority was one of her three main concerns.[53]

Renaming the County Annex Building

In July of 2022 the Rio Arriba County Commission unanimously voted to rename the Rio Arriba County Annex Building in Española the Emilio Naranjo Building. Naranjo's nephew, Rio Arriba County Commissioner Alex Naranjo, introduced the resolution calling for the name change in December, shortly before he left office, stating in *The New Mexican*, "He was a public servant for 50 years. My uncle was a legend in Northern New Mexico. I'm very proud of him."

I spoke with Ike about Emilio Naranjo, Alex Naranjo, and a family's legacy that impacts the people of Rio Arriba County far beyond a building at the county complex. Alex and his brother, Nick Naranjo, nephews of Emilio, have been engaged in power plays for years in their various county government positions. I asked Ike why he thinks this side of the family, Alex and Nick's side, has been the one to perpetuate the patron system. "Emilio was omnipotent for so long, they probably think they're entitled, they're royalty. All this stuff is old history with Emilio, but wounds, even though they're old, they're still there. And they're reopened when these guys continue to be unaccountable."

Nick Naranjo's position, as chairman of the Jemez Mountains Electric Co-op board, had been on the front page for months as co-op members challenged the utility's contract with Tri-State and his authoritarian rule over a severely divided board. Naranjo and his cohort consistently rejected members' appeals to cancel its contract with Tri-State, which provides primarily fossil fuel energy, and contract with a source that supplies more renewable energy. After the year's June elections Naranjo led a movement to remove opposition board member Bruce Duran (claiming he lived out of his district, a false claim), forcing Duran and Patrick Herrera, who ran for a different position on the board on a reform slate, and three other member-owners of the co-op, to file suit. (Herrera also contested his loss, claiming board member Lucas Córdova was the one who didn't live in his district.) Another group, JMEC Trustees 4 Change, had a petition to "Take Back Our

Co-op" and was raising money for Duran's legal defense.

Longtime Dixon resident Stan Crawford, who won a seat on the board for District 5 in June as part of the reform slate, submitted a letter to the board claiming that only the membership of the co-op can remove a board member and that the board elected officers and appointments at its July 21st meeting without a quorum.

People were not going to take the renaming of the county building lying down. On August 27, they headed to Tierra Amarilla to protest the name change resolution. But Rio Arriba County Commissioner Danny Garcia's comment—"I feel your pain, but as long as the patron fixes my road, he's got my vote"—about summed up the commission's response to Ike and Carol Miller's testimony.[54] Ike told the commission, "I stood up against Naranjo politically, not personally," because of the tactic of fear he employed to keep his power. "People had to kneel down at the altar of Emilio Naranjo." Ike told his story about when Naranjo deployed his deputies against him to try to quiet his opposition. In a chilling delivery he again told the story of how they planted drugs at his house while Naranjo put out a contract on his life. In self-defense, he disarmed the off-duty sheriff's deputy who challenged him to a fight. He was arrested and sent to the New Mexico Penitentiary where he was beaten by the guards.

Carol Miller, of Ojo Sarco, is a longtime health specialist and activist who, as I wrote about in Chapter One, was the Executive Director of La Clinica del Pueblo de Rio Arriba in Tierra Amarilla after Ike's tenure there. Naranjo targeted the clinic as a community stronghold of the Tierra Amarilla Land Grant and La Raza Unida, and Ike and Miller had to sue the county to force it to fund ambulance service and road maintenance at the clinic from the mill levy (the county settled with a large one-time cash payment and guaranteed share of the mill levy).

Miller read a statement signed by Wilfredo Vigil, another long time norteño activist. She asked the county to "find a name for the county complex in Española that unites our community," that looks forward, not backward, to someone who caused so much pain and who so many had to sue to hold to account. She identified the people at the commission meeting who were harmed by Naranjo: Ike DeVargas, Larry Miller, Alan Siegal (who Naranjo arrested on a misdemeanor charge and illegally delivered to a federal prison in Texas) and Moises Morales. Morales told stories of being shot at and, like Ike, framed by a drug plant. He was also targeted, along with Pedro Archuleta, by the FBI as having connections to a militant Puerto Rican liberation group, all unsubstantiated. Miller asked the commissioners to be a "new face" for our children. She also referenced a letter by Richard Rosenstock asking the commission to reconsider its decision to name the building after someone who violated so many people's civil rights. In the letter he laid out the history of the cases against Moises and Ike, both of whom he represented, and all of which were dismissed or settled in favor of the defendants.

Commission Chairman Garcia, whom I paraphrased earlier, went on at length that while he acknowledged that Naranjo's illegal activities had hurt many people, it could be excused by what is essentially patronage, i.e., fixing someone's road for their vote and support. Garcia was challenged by Larry Miller, who told him that Naranjo didn't get his road fixed, our tax dollars did.

Commissioner Leo Jaramillo asked County Manager Tomás Compos if there was a process the county must follow to officially name county buildings or sites. Compos cited examples of when public figures had donated money to have a park or other site named for them, but this was the first time the county had passed a resolution to rename a building. Jaramillo suggested that if resolutions were promulgated by the commission it would be a good idea to hold public hearings before action was taken. Ike responded, "How about just keep the name Rio Arriba County Annex Building, which represents the citizens of Rio Arriba County." He reminded the commissioners that the state was forced to remove former state legislator Manny Aragon's name from a government building after he was convicted and sent to prison for conspiracy to defraud the state. In that vein, let's not forget the number of museums and cultural sites named for the Purdue Pharma Sackler family under indictment for false advertising of opioids, or the cancer centers and art facilities named for the recently deceased David Koch, an oil and corporate magnate largely responsible for climate disruption, a condition he denied.

The three commissioners (the third county commissioner, James Martinez, who spoke less than Garcia and Jaramillo, is the son-in-law of Española pastor Michael Naranjo, who is Emilio Naranjo's nephew) said they would "discuss" what the protesters presented and decide later whether they would leave the building named for Naranjo or reconsider the resolution.

North Central Again

Five months later, on Tuesday, January 25, 2022, Ike again addressed the Rio Arriba County Commission about the North Central Waste Management Authority, but this time the meeting was held at the Emilio Naranjo Administrative Building in Española, which, as of the writing of this book, retains that contested name. While not an auspicious setting for this second attempt to convince the county to either fix the inequities of North Central or do away with the Ordinance that established it, Commissioners James Martinez, Christine Bustos, and Moises Morales (Bustos and Morales were newly elected commissioners), along with County Manager Lucia Sanchez, readily acknowledged that the solid waste system was not working and needed to be fixed.

During his presentation, Ike stated that there were 1,038 delinquent accounts; neither Rio Arriba County nor the North Central Authority knew how many of these delinquencies were due to the party being deceased or no longer living at the address. The county had failed to follow Section 10 of Ordinance 97-04 that requires the county manager to file notice of delinquency before issuing liens and to hear any complaints or grievances within 15 days. Without a code enforcement officer to investigate these delinquencies, there was no way for the county to follow proper procedure.

Ike read from the opening paragraph of the Ordinance: "The ordinance is intended to eliminate illegal dumping and accumulation of solid waste, to preserve and protect public health and the environment, and institute administrative procedures to effectively manage solid waste generated in the unincorporated areas of Rio Arriba County." He then passed out photos of what the county actually looks like, with garbage dumped in arroyos and trash accumulated in residents' yards.

Ike asked the commissioners to get rid of the liens against county citizens and then start from scratch: If the North Central Authority is not doing its job, let's figure out a better way to tackle the solid waste problems in Rio Arriba County. To emphasize that North Central was indeed "not doing its job" he read from a newspaper article that stated, "If this [North Central] was a commercial entity I'd say the Authority is bankrupt." Ike pointed out that between 2008 and 2012 Rio Arriba County budgeted $3.8 million for the Authority, which he referred to as taxation without representation. "Nobody voted for this Authority."

This time around Ike got a swift response from Commissioner Morales. "We developed the Ordinance and we need to come up with the solutions to this situation." He also claimed that the current trash situation was partly the fault of the Forest Service, which closed its dumps on the federal lands that constitute much of Rio Arriba County. The other commissioners agreed that the Ordinance needed to be upgraded but hedged that the other parties to the Joint Powers Agreement (JPA) should also address the issues.

County Manager Lucia Sanchez, who had only served in this position for seven months (previously the County Planner), provided the most robust response to Ike's complaints and left him and his supporters feeling that appropriate actions might actually be taken. She told Ike that as County Planner she had a code enforcement officer who made sure residences were tied to trash accounts, and now, as County Manager, she would work to provide adequate code enforcement.

"The Ordinance is arbitrary and capricious and unenforceable," she said, and gives too much power to the county manager. She and her team have given it a "broad brush" review and now need to figure out how to dissolve it with the JPA partners. "We are not in the business of taking people's land."[55]

A Grand Jury Indictment

Fast forward to August of 2023. The grand jury empaneled by Ike's citizen petition finally alleged the North Central Solid Waste Authority committed "malfeasance, misappropriation of funds and unlawful liens" and called for its indictment, citing "fake billing for services not rendered." The jury also indicted Rio Arriba County Chairman Alex Naranjo (re-elected to the county commission) and former Rio Arriba County Manager Tomás Campos on charges of perjury (lying before the grand jury). The Attorney General's Office also announced it intended to investigate on the recommendation of the grand jury.

The coronavirus wasn't the only thing that had slowed down the jury process, first convened in 2019. First Judicial Assistant District Attorney Douglas Wood tried to halt the grand jury process, citing a New Mexico Supreme Court order that limited the scope of grand jury cases state prosecutors could pursue during the pandemic. But Judge Lidyard claimed the Supreme Court's order was aimed at curbing prosecutorial overuse of grand juries, not one like this against the Authority, and finally, the grand jury released its findings. Ike believed that Assistant DA Wood was hostile to the idea of the grand jury from the get-go, telling him he thought it should be a civil case. But that would entail dealing with 1,000 or more property liens on a case-by-case basis. He added, "I think Wood tried to nullify this special grand jury because it allows citizens to investigate public officials. I feel very vindicated. People told me I was like Sancho Panza tilting at windmills."

Ike requested to be on the August 2023 agenda of the Rio Arriba County Commission meeting to see what action the commissioners would take to meet the grand jury's recommendation that board members be removed from their posts. "I could circulate a recall petition if the DA or AG doesn't remove Naranjo and the commission. But you know," he told me, "if they cancel all the liens and start a trash pick-up from scratch, I won't bother taking any more actions against politicians." No one was making bets on that.

Relocation of Juan de Oñate Statue

And it didn't happen, of course. While waiting for the Rio Arriba County Commission and the First Judicial District Attorney's office to act on the grand jury's indictments, another conflict involving County Chair Alex Naranjo raised its ugly head. Apparently, Naranjo decided to relocate the statue of conquistador Juan de Oñate to the Rio Arriba County Complex in Española. This is the statue that had been removed from its position at the former Oñate Monument and Visitor's Center in Alcalde in 2020 during the wave of toppled Confederate and racist statues across the country.

I stood next to Ike and his grandson Andres at that 2020 celebration (Ike was Andres's legal guardian, explained in the next chapter). When the last Red Nation speaker cried out, "We're coming for you, DeVargas," referring to the statue of Don Diego de Vargas in Cathedral Park in Santa Fe, the look on Andres's face was startling. "Are they coming for us, grandpa?" he asked Ike.

Ike explained to Andres that no, they were referring to the Santa Fe statue. But he also had to explain why a statue named DeVargas was in Santa Fe in the first place, and that although they share a name with

Andres and Ike

a Spanish conquistador, they share a much more complicated genealogy of Mexicano, Indio, Nuevomexicano, and Chicano, the intersection of all those who make up the northern New Mexico community.

Although the celebration at the Oñate Monument and Visitor's Center was led by the Red Nation, founded in Albuquerque several years ago, this site has been the center of controversy within the larger norteño community for many years, at the hands of Emilio Naranjo. Naranjo saw himself as a descendant of Oñate, not only via Spanish blood but by dominion rule over those he deemed inferior. The building and statue were largely seen as a boondoggle by those who had to come up with the money to maintain it and an affront to those oppressed by both Naranjo and Oñate.

Rio Arriba County may have turned a protest into a celebration by taking down the statue, but it failed miserably to disassociate itself from the Naranjo legacy. In an issued statement, County Manager Tomás Campos said he ordered its removal for "safe keeping" after the county learned of the planned demonstration and possible "destruction or damage" to the statue. In a separate statement, County Commissioner Leo Jaramillo said that the commission welcomed a discussion with county residents about the future of the statue, but Jaramillo would soon leave the commission; he won the Democratic primary for state senate.

Kurly Tlapoyawa, an archaeologist, author, and ethnohistorian, takes a critical look at the Oñate myth in his blog Unseennm.org.

"The hispanos view their veneration of Juan de Oñate as a matter of European birthright, and perceive any criticism of Oñate and the parade held in his honor as an assault on their culture. And therein lies the problem: by framing Oñate as the embodiment of their culture, Oñate supporters have painted themselves into an ideological corner, creating an intractable situation in which even the slightest compromise would be seen as complete cultural surrender. In their minds, admitting that Oñate was a piece of shit is tantamount to admitting that their culture is also shit."[56]

There is a disconnect in the Indigenous community as well. The governor of Ohkay Owingeh, Ron Lovato, allied himself in a letter with State Representative District 40 Joseph Sanchez (who ran unsuccessfully in the Democrat primary for US Representative), a conservative Catholic: "The actions taken today at the Oñate Monument and Visitor's Center, unfortunately, unfolded without consultation with Ohkay Owingeh, its members, or that of the greater surrounding Hispano communities." The letter went on to say what others argue, that these statues teach us our history, and we should learn from it, not erase it. "For hundreds of years, our communities have lived in harmony and continue to look ahead and plan to the benefit of the generations to come."[57]

In a comment regarding Tlapoyawa's essay, Richard Rosenstock suggested that, in addition to the arguments over Spanish purity, "sentiments that arise in northern New Mexico are, in many cases, coming from a more complicated place that includes resentment and anger over the increasing feelings of marginalization. This seems obvious in Santa Fe where the entire downtown was lost to long-time residents long ago, and families that lived in the city for many generations can no longer live there."[58]

PHOTO BY LUIS PEÑA

Oñate coming down

A good place to explore the genesis of this loss is *The Language of Blood: The Making of Spanish-American Identity in New Mexico 1880s-1930s*, by John N. Nieto-Phillips. Nieto-Phillips traces the metaphor of identity as the language of blood purity, or limpieza de sangre, from the 1880s through the 1930s.[59] Two basic factors fueled its creation: Anglo tourism and settlement that exploited the Spanish colonial past to implement Manifest Destiny; and Nuevomexicanos own use of Spanish purity, as opposed to Mexicano or metizaje, as a defense against political and social marginalization by this same Anglo settlement.

In another book that looks at the more recent gentrification of Santa Fe, the *Myth of Santa Fe: Creating a Modern Regional Tradition*, author Chris Wilson lays out the story of how in the 1980s the Anglo newcomers undertook a public campaign to project Santa Fe to the world as an exotic tourist destination using tri-culturalism—Indian, Spanish, and Anglo—to create what he terms a "successful illusion of authenticity" that commodified Indio and Hispano cultures. The result, just as Rosenstock notes, was displacement and ethnic animosity.[60]

In a press release Ike, and Luis Peña, a younger activist from Española whose father was a Servilleta Plaza neighbor and friend of Ike for many years, invited members of the local media and the public to a press conference on Monday, September 25th, at 12 noon in front of the Rio Arriba County Complex—not the Annex that was renamed the Emilio Naranjo County Building—"to address a matter of significant community concern about the decision to relocate the statue of conquistador, Juan de Oñate, and to discuss the grand jury indictment of the North Central Solid Waste Authority (NCSWA) for malfeasance, fraud, incorrect billing and misappropriation of public funds. This statue represents a man not worthy of honoring. Oñate was tried, convicted, and exiled by Spain for his crimes against the Pueblos and his own people. Rio Arriba County Commissioner Alex Naranjo knows that this statue will continue to create controversy and that it invites continued harm on Native people. The statue's very presence is an act of violence on the descendant communities who live in Rio Arriba."

In response, the Rio Arriba County Manager issued his own press release on September 27 "postponing" the planned raising of the Juan de Oñate statue at the county complex. Native Americans and Nuevomexicanos had been holding vigil since the press conference against the movement of the statue from storage to display.

Luis and Ike were also working to draft a recall petition to remove Rio Arriba County Commissioner President Alex Naranjo, who, from all accounts, ordered the statue's resurrection without consultation with the other commissioners or the county manager. Luis and Ike also held Naranjo accountable for the county's abuse of power in placing liens on the properties under the auspices of the North Central Solid Waste Authority.

Juan de Oñate statue at the Oñate Monument and Visitors Center

On September 28, however, all hell broke loose at the county complex vigil when a young man in a Make America Great Again hat, who had been harassing the Native Americans and Nuevomexicanos gathered in front of the county complex, shot Native activist Jacob Johns in the stomach. Johns, from Spokane, Washington, had been in Española to attend a conference and had joined the local, peaceful protestors who had spent several nights in front of the complex to offer food and assistance to the attendees. The shooter, Ryan Martinez of Sandia Park, New Mexico, was chased down and arrested. (Martinez pleaded no contest to aggravated battery and aggravated assault with a deadly weapon and was sentenced to 9.5 years, which includes a firearm enhancement.) Jacob Johns recovered after extensive surgery and sued Martinez and his family, who failed to prevent the shooting, and Rio Arriba County officials, who failed to provide a safe environment.

In December of 2023 the First Judicial District Attorney's office turned the North Central Waste Management Authority grand jury case over to 13th Judicial District Attorney Barbara Romo, citing it had a "conflict of interest" and couldn't prosecute the case. Romo then dismissed the case, claiming that the grand jury had overstepped its authority by looking into issues that weren't raised in the initial petition that Ike filed. As reported in the *Santa Fe New Mexican*, she specifically cited the perjury charges against Naranjo and Campos that weren't included in Ike's petition or the court's "order to convene." Ike was incredulous over this reasoning. "How the hell would I know that Alex and Tomas would perjure themselves in front of the grand jury!"[61]

Ike believed the First Judicial District Attorney's office under District Attorney Mary Carmack-Altwies was incompetent and filed a complaint with the New Mexico Bar Association. "This damn district attorney has screwed up everything. Where did she get this prosecutor [Romo]? The grand jury was critical of the DA's office from the get go when it refused to provide information the jury wanted and even received inaccurate information."

The Attorney General's Office was still conducting a civil investigation into North Central Solid Waste Authority, but Ike noted that the AG's office had been requesting the names of witnesses who testified before the grand jury from him. "They have the right to get the entire record of the grand jury. Why are they asking me to provide them with that information?"

Recall of Alex Naranjo

While extremely disappointed by the dismissal of the grand jury indictments, Ike proceeded with his recall petition of Rio Arriba County Commissioner Alex Naranjo over the grand jury indictment and his attempt to relocate the statue of Juan de Oñate at the Rio Arriba County Complex in Española. After every local district judge recused themselves from hearing the case, it was assigned to Second Judicial District Judge Benjamin Chavez (in Albuquerque), and Naranjo was served a summons. Another delay ensued when Ike's initial complaint, originally filed in October of 2023, had to be amended and filed by attorney Richard Rosenstock.

Then, in another annoying delay, District Judge Benjamin Chavez resigned from his job on Friday, January 19. Ike was concerned that all these delays would allow the issue to fade from the public's memory and would make it harder, if and when the judge found probable cause to allow him to proceed with the recall, to obtain the requisite number of signatures. Only voters in Naranjo's District 2 could sign the recall petition, and Ike estimated he'd have to obtain at least 33 percent of them. Time was also of the essence because a recall can't be conducted within 180 days of an election, in which Naranjo was running for re-election. Both Ike and Rosenstock were unsure whether the case could be assigned to another sitting judge or if they'd have to wait until the governor appointed a replacement for Chavez.

It was a situation that made one wonder if there was an agenda guiding these delays in a recall of a public figure, just as the First Judicial District made it clear it didn't want to investigate Rio Arriba County elected officials despite a grand jury indictment. But Ike said he was prepared to proceed with the recall if and when a judge decided the case could move forward.

Finally, a court hearing on Ike's recall petition of Naranjo was held on May 3 at the First District Courthouse in Santa Fe. A new judge, Marie Ward, was assigned to the case to determine whether he could proceed with his recall petition of Commissioner Naranjo based on the grand jury indictment of the North Central Solid Waste Authority and Naranjo's attempt to relocate the statue of Juan de Oñate at the Rio Arriba County Complex in Española.

Rosenstock represented Ike at the hearing and presented evidence to demonstrate that "probable cause exists to support these allegations against Commissioner Naranjo and to thus allow the citizens of Rio Arriba County to decide whether a recall election should be held." Naranjo was represented at the hearing by his own legal counsel, who failed to call any witnesses.

I wrote an article in *La Jicarita* about the hearing that started with this reference: "I don't know how many norteños have been watching "The Curse," a TV streaming show that takes place in Española, but "The Cringe" would be a better title based on the feeling I had watching the clueless gringo couple build so-called eco-housing that even 'poor Nuevomexicanos can afford.' You're *supposed* to cringe as their antics satirize gentrification, identity politics, the media, and 'wokeness.'"

That cringe feeling carried over to the four-hour hearing in First District Court on Tuesday, March 19, when Rio Arriba County officialdom's dysfunction was exposed in excruciating lies, malfeasance, and dereliction of duty.[62]

Highlighting the hearing was the riveting testimony of County Manager Jeremy Maestas, who, under Rosenstock's questioning, claimed he alone made the decision to reinstate the Oñate statue, citing public support from Española Fiesta Council members and those who support this controversial celebration of the conquistador. However, Rosenstock provided copies of emails in which Maestas said the commission had made the decision. Maestas also admitted he'd never read the grand jury report on the North Central Solid Waste Authority or spoken about it with Naranjo.

PHOTO BY PHAEDRA HAYWOOD.
Copyright © 2024 The New Mexican, Inc. Reprinted with permission. All rights reserved

Alex Naranjo and Ike at the hearing

Once again, the First District Attorney's Office showed its bias against the petition by trying to squelch Assistant District Attorney Douglas Wood's summons to vouch for the North Central grand jury's authenticity. Wood had already failed to pursue prosecution of the grand jury's indictment of North Central and Naranjo. Once Rosenstock pointed out that only documents released by the grand jury would be used in the hearing, the judge declared that the court could proceed without Wood's testimony to see if "probable cause exists" to move forward with the recall petition. Woods, who had his own lawyer with him, got up and left.

On the witness stand, Ike told the court he had supported Naranjo's 2022 re-election campaign—Naranjo previously served on the commission several times—because Naranjo told him he would instigate a forensic audit of North Central once he was elected (for misuse of funds and illegal liens on people's properties). "I have no animus towards Mr. Naranjo," Ike said. In fact, they grew up together in the same Española neighborhood. Ike also told the court that he first heard of the county's plan to move the Oñate statue to the county complex on KDCE Radio in a Naranjo interview. He continued that it was Naranjo's uncle, Rio Arriba County patron, Emilio Naranjo, who first commissioned the statue of Oñate in the 1990s that was erected at the Oñate Monument and Visitor's Center in Alcalde. Ike was there, along with many others, when that statue was taken down in 2020 and put into storage at the county.

Nathana Bird, a member of Ohkay Owingeh and Associate Director of Tewa Women United, learned about the planned September 28, 2023 installment of the statue on a Facebook page "Invitation to Attend." There was never any public hearing about this event, which, in her opinion, had caused Indigenous people "historical trauma" and was like "ripping the band-aid off a wound." She also expressed anger that public funds had been used to erect the pedestal on which the statue would stand. She, along with her partner and many others from the Pueblo, were at the county complex in peaceful protest when Ryan Martinez, a MAGA (Make American Great Again) supporter, pulled a gun and shot Jacob Johns.

Luis Peña was also called as a witness. Luis worked with Ike on the recall petition and applied his technical skills to make the public records requests that revealed the Maestas emails (some of these emails were to Ryan Martinez, who queried Maestas about the statue). He testified that Commissioner Naranjo told him he made the decision to reinstate the statue in a personal conversation. Peña also happily copped to a Facebook post—provided by Naranjo's attorney—calling out Maestas in rather colorful language, but later apologized.

The final witness called—Naranjo's attorney didn't call any witnesses—was Rio Arriba County Sheriff Billy Merrifield, who also received an email from Maestas saying that the commission had made the decision to erect the statue in front of the county complex. Merrifield testified that he was not in favor of this decision because he was concerned about the possibility of violence due to the controversy surrounding the statue. He reached out to other law enforcement agencies to plan for increased presence at the installation. It was "great news" to him when it was cancelled, and he attended the meeting when two commissioners voted for the cancellation, with Naranjo voting to proceed.

Ironically, the violence Sheriff Merrifield worried about happened because the statue *didn't* go up, not because it did. What that says about those who view Oñate as a positive cultural icon is hypocritical, and what it says about the decisions made by Rio Arriba County officials is disturbing. If the judge ruled that Ike could proceed with his petition he'd have to gather approximately 1,200 signatures of voters to proceed with a recall election.

Running for County Commissioner

Just as Ike's recall petition came before Judge Ward, he threw his hat in the ring for Rio Arriba County Commissioner, District 3, the seat currently held by Moises Morales, in March of 2023.

Ike's single poster for county commissioner

Here's what he posted on Facebook.

If elected the following are my platform goals:

1. To serve one 4-year term and then pass the torch to a younger person, preferably a woman in the mid 40s to mid 50s group in order to provide a gender balance on the board.

2. To explore the feasibility of expanding the board to 5 members in order to give better representation to the citizens of Rio Arriba County. Most New Mexico Counties have 5 members.

3. To make sure all County business is conducted in the open, to provide the transparency that citizens need and deserve to be properly informed.

4. That all major positions (E.G.) County Manager, are advertised so that the County can hire the most qualified person to do the job for the COUNTY.

5. To review and update the arbitrary, capricious, and antiquated Rio Arriba Solid Waste Ordinance that has resulted in the terrible situation that is the North Central Solid Waste Authority.

6. To review and possibly repeal other Ordinances that have been enacted without the resources to be enforced. These kinds of ordinances lead to citizens' disrespect for the law and eventually to the disrespect for the law makers as well.

7. I pledge to host town hall community meetings in different locations in the 3rd District in order to hear voters' concerns, criticisms, and recommendations to improve County services.

8. To encourage younger citizens to participate in the political arena of our County and State. They are the future!!

Richard Rosenstock and I tried to persuade him not to do it. Both of us worried that he was under enough pressure with the impending recall (if approved), his responsibilities to his grandson Andres, and his health. He'd survived a mild heart attack in 2023 and had numerous chronic conditions that required trips to the VA Hospital, which meant a trip to Albuquerque, and various other doctors and treatments.

But Ike was fed up with Morales's failure to stand up as a county commissioner and do what Naranjo had failed to do about the North Central Solid Waste Authority. He met with Morales numerous times and urged him to bring the issue before the commission to either amend or rescind the Authority's ordinance and start over with a county-run solid waste program. But as Ike often complained to me,

"Moises is just putting in his time until he can retire on a government pension. He doesn't give a shit about the county."

This is strong language about someone who was his political comrade and lifelong compadre. Here's the explanation that Ike released:

"Many people are asking why I would challenge my old friend Moises Morales for the County Commission seat in the Rio Arriba County 3rd district, a position he has held for 12 years. The reasons are that he has consistently refused to lead, being in effect nothing more than a rubber stamp. I guess I should not be surprised because as a member of La Raza Unida for more than 15 years Moises was always ready to speak at the rallies, participate in the protests and marches, but always declined to be the chairman. As such, he never organized a rally, protest or march but just got his name recognition as a speaker.

Moises and Ike at a Rio Arriba County Function in earlier days

"The same is true as a commissioner. He has been tagged repeatedly to be the chairman and has always declined the responsibility, preferring to take credit for accomplishments but not accepting responsibility for failures such as the North Central Solid Waste Authority debacle. Despite always protesting the federal government's taking of the community land grants, his name is now on the ordinance that has placed unlawful, arbitrary, and capricious liens on citizens' homes and properties. He repeatedly told me that the liens should not have been levied on the people, that the word lien was inserted into the language of the ordinance only to scare people into participating in the program. When I asked why he did nothing to reverse what has been happening, he blamed the other commissioners for not supporting him. When I asked him to introduce a motion at a regular commission meeting so that he could make his position clear to the citizens and voters, he falsely stated 'only the chairman can advance a motion.' When I asked him if he had read the Grand Jury Report that laid out the corruption and cruel and unlawful placing of liens on citizens' homes and properties, he stated that he had not.

"In my view this is a clear dereliction of his duty to the citizens he is supposed to represent and a reason why he should not be reelected to the job. I feel strongly that the voters of the third district of Rio Arriba County deserve more than a rubber stamp and a person who is willing and capable of assuming the job of chairman when called upon. This in a nutshell is why I humbly ask the voters for their vote in this race!"

The Recall Continues

In a decision released on May 2, District Court Judge Marie Ward ordered that Ike's petition to recall Rio Arriba County Commissioner Alex Naranjo was granted permission to proceed. The issues raised in the recall petition were: 1) the findings of a grand jury indictment of North Central Solid Waste Authority and Commissioner Naranjo of "malfeasance or misfeasance in office and/or violation of the oath of office"; and 2) violation of the Open Meetings Act (OMA) in deciding to reinstate the statue of conquistador Juan de Oñate at the Rio Arriba County Complex. Judge Ward's order is based only on the second issue:

"Violating the New Mexico Open Meetings Act by making a decision outside of an open, public meeting to place the statue of Juan de

Oñate at the Rio Arriba County Office Complex or acting in concert with others to do so."[63]

While Ike still believed the findings of the grand jury indictment of North Central Solid Waste Authority and Commissioner Naranjo remained valid, he was pleased that the court's decision now allowed him to move forward with his petition. The court decision affirmed Ike's petition claim that "Probable cause supports the allegation that Commissioner Naranjo violated the New Mexico Open Meetings Act by making a decision outside of an open public meeting to place a statue of Juan de Oñate in a public location." The judge found that violations of the OMA can constitute Malfeasance or Misfeasance and "that the conduct was done with the improper motive of shielding a controversial decision from public scrutiny." She also found that County Manager Jeremy Maestas's testimony that he was the official who made the decision to install the statue "lack[ed] credibility."

The Court found that Ike and Rosenstock didn't establish probable cause to support the allegation that Commissioner Naranjo committed perjury when he testified before the grand jury in May 2023 regarding the North Central Solid Waste Authority. The judge found that the grand jury's report, submitted as evidence of Naranjo's perjury, needed additional evidence, such as documents and the testimony of multiple witnesses that were not presented to the Court (First District Attorney's Office showed its bias against the findings of the grand jury by squelching Assistant DA Douglas Wood's summons to vouch for the North Central grand jury's authenticity). She also dismissed the petition's claim of Naranjo's dereliction of duty, incompetency, and negligence because they "are not grounds for recall."

Alex Naranjo's attorney filed an appeal of the District Court decision allowing the recall petition to proceed later in May. The appeal went to the New Mexico Supreme Court, which could affirm the district court ruling or ask for a response from Rosenstock, additional briefs, or set a hearing in its own court. In a matter of days, the court sent Rosenstock a request for a response, which was due in three days.

Did the Supreme Court then expedite a hearing before the June 5th primary election? Of course not. Just as everything else concerning this case had been previously delayed, the Supreme Court decision lingered for more than a month while the election transpired and Ike garnered approximately 26 percent of the vote (but a majority in his district of Ojo Caliente and La Madera) for county commissioner. Voter turnout was abysmal; of 21,399 eligible voters in Rio Arriba County, only 5,576 ballots were cast. Considering that he'd declared his candidacy only several months previously and spent very little money, he was both proud that he'd made the effort and relieved that he didn't have to take away any more time from the responsibility of raising his grandson.

Chapter Seven

Carmela DeVargas

Carmela DeVargas, Ike's 34-year-old daughter, died on November 9, 2019, as a result of failure at the Santa Fe County Adult Detention Facility to afford her the necessary medical treatment to save her life. Carmela was being held in the Santa Fe Facility on an alleged probation violation and became ill due to the jail's failure to treat her for Opioid Use Disorder that resulted in infections that rendered her quadriplegic and on life support (meningoencephalitis, epidural abscess, and sepsis caused by Methicillin-resistant Staphylococcus aureus or MRSA). Carmela contracted these infections from either the filthy conditions at the Santa Fe County Adult Detention Facility or from a dirty needle she used to self-medicate while an inmate there. She languished at the jail for weeks without adequate medical attention, despite the Facility's knowledge of her Opioid Use Disorder and the risks of withdrawal and medical complications associated with it. She had called her father and sister, Elisa DeVargas, numerous times to complain of fever and headaches and told them the guards ignored or mocked her when she tried to get medical help. Her condition became critical and she was transferred to Christus St. Vincent Regional Medical Center, where she was shackled, both arm and legs, while in the ICU, intubated and on life support. Officers refused the hospital's request to remove the shackles for a full week until the county dismissed her criminal charges and she was transferred to the University of New Mexico Hospital for a final evaluation. Always cognizant of her condition, she chose to terminate life support and ended her life.

Rex Corcoran, Jr., also held at the Santa Fe County Adult Detention Facility on an alleged probation violation, died four days after Carmela of organ failure due to sepsis. Rex had been in the Facility for only seven days when he was transferred to Christus St. Vincent Regional Medical Center. His mother, Susie Schmitt, said that she tried unsuccessfully to reach her son by phone and never saw him alive again; she had to make the decision to take him off life support at the hospital. "You don't go to jail healthy and come out dead. You go to jail for a minor offense that does not deserve the death penalty."

Rex and Carmela

Grand Jury Request

"I decided if the law enforcement of the state doesn't want to do its job, it's time for the citizens to take the law into their own hands, and I'm not talking about violence."[64] With these words, Ike opened a press conference on Saturday, February 8, to announce that he and Susie Schmitt were starting a petition drive to empanel a grand jury to investigate the deaths of their children, caused by "misfeasance, malfeasance, and other crimes that may have been committed by their county government and its agency, the Santa Fe County Adult Detention Facility." Dozens of others have died at the Facility due to unsanitary conditions and lack of health care.

Ike initially asked the Santa Fe County District Attorney to investigate Carmela's death but was told he had to file a police report. The Santa Fe County Sheriff told him he couldn't conduct the investigation because, as a county employee, it would constitute a conflict of interest. Ike was referred to the State Police, where he was told his complaint would be sent up the chain of command. He didn't hear back from law enforcement. Ike told the crowd, "My efforts to get the New Mexico State Police to investigate what I consider to be the negligent homicide of my daughter, Carmela DeVargas, the death of Rex Corcoran, and many others at the Santa Fe County Adult Detention Facility have been ignored. Therefore, it is imperative that the citizens of the City and County of Santa Fe exercise their constitutional rights to petition for the empanelment of a citizens' Grand Jury to investigate misfeasance, malfeasance, and other crimes that may have been committed."

Susie Schmitt and Ike

The state's constitution allows someone to impanel a grand jury with a petition "signed by not less than the greater of two hundred registered voters or two percent of the registered voters of the county." While the Santa Fe County Clerk would have to verify qualified Santa Fe County registered voters' names on the petition, Ike and Schmitt encouraged everyone who cares about criminal justice reform to sign the petition as a signal to the County that it was time for it to investigate its Detention Facility. Richard Rosenstock supplied him with links to dozens of criminal complaints, tort claims, and an ongoing class action lawsuit (filed in 2017), Armendariz et al.-v.-Santa Fe County, documenting appalling conditions and abuse by guards at the Detention Facility. Ike told the crowd, "We want accountability," not settlements (up to $500,000) that do nothing to get rid of the "crap" at the top, not just the abusive guards who "mocked my daughter."

The American Civil Liberties Union (ACLU) also spoke at the press conference to announce that its organization is working with state legislators to reduce sentences for substance abuse cases. Rosenstock told the crowd that "This is a political issue. The Santa Fe County Commission should be interested in knowing what's going on in its jail. Get on the commission agenda to force them to look into these abuses." Several activists in the crowd said they were organizing to do just that; appear before the Commission to demand accountability.

Ike also filed a formal complaint against the Chief Medical Officer at the Detention Facility and planned to file a lawsuit as well. The New Mexico Medical Board agreed to investigate his complaint, saying it would take 90 days to do so.

Ike told the crowd he would continue to collect signatures for the next few months. Seventy-eight people signed the petition at the press conference and took copies to pass out to family, friends, and colleagues.

This is the petition:

> PETITION FOR GRAND JURY INVESTIGATION
>
> We the undersigned voters of Santa Fe County, hereby petition the judges of the First Judicial District Court, pursuant to Article II, Section 14 of the New Mexico State Constitution, to convene a Grand Jury to investigate acts of malfeasance, misfeasance, and any other illegal act committed by any individuals associated with or employed by the Santa Fe County Adult Detention Facility and the County of Santa Fe. These other acts include the denial of medical care by the willful and deliberate indifference of the medical staff, the mocking and dehumanizing of inmates in their care by guards employed at the Santa Fe County Adult Detention Facility that have resulted in the recent death of Carmela DeVargas on November 9, 2019, and the death of Rex Cochran on November 13, 2019, as well many other inmate deaths, multiple law suits (and settlements), and pending tort claims.

Ike, Schmitt, family, and friends circulated the petition over the course of several months, hoping to get 2,000 Santa Fe County signatories. They also circulated the petition throughout northern New Mexico, as many of those mistreated at the Facility are from various norteño communities.

Demonstration at the Santa Fe County Adult Detention Facility
March 2020

Flowers for Carmela

On December 20, 2019, Rosenstock filed a Notice of Tort Claim for the Carmela DeVargas estate. The estate includes Carmela's two children, Andres, who lives with Ike, his legal guardian, and Maria, who was adopted by another family.

Richard Rosenstock, Attorney at Law
1121 Paseo de Peralta
Santa Fe, NM 87501
505-988-5324 (voice) 505-989-4844 (fax)
Richard.Rosenstock@gmail.com

Geraldine Salazar
Santa Fe County Clerk
102 Grant Avenue
Santa Fe, New Mexico 87501

December 20, 2019

Re: Notice of Tort Claim—The Estate of Carmela DeVargas, Andres DeVargas and Maria DeVargas

Dear Ms. Salazar,

On behalf of The Estate of Carmela DeVargas, deceased, Andres DeVargas, a minor and Maria DeVargas, a minor please accept this letter as official notice of claim under Section 41-4-1 NMSA ("The Tort Claims Act"). It is claimed that the Santa Fe County Detention Center negligently and/or recklessly failed to provide adequate medical services and/or treatment to Carmela DeVargas while she was a pre-trial detainee there during the September 19- October 20, 2019 time period and that as a direct and proximate result Ms. DeVargas died on or about November 9, 2019.

It is further claimed by the Estate that Ms. DeVargas was subjected to continuing unreasonable seizures of her person when she was kept in restraints by Detention Center personnel during the eight days she was at Christus St. Vincent's Hospital. Ms. DeVargas was a quadriplegic during virtually her entire time there, could not move her arms and legs, and keeping her in restraints was, under the totality of the circumstances, totally unnecessary and unreasonable and constituted the County's final degradation of her person. The Estate claims this conduct violated the New Mexico Constitution, Article II, Section 10.

A claim for loss of consortium is also asserted for Andres DeVargas, the minor son of Carmela DeVargas, and Maria DeVargas, the minor daughter of Ms. DeVargas,

I ask that you provide this letter to the City Attorney as soon as possible.

Sincerely,

s/Richard Rosenstock

s/Daniel Yohalem

New Mexico Civil Rights Act

On February 8, 2021, Ike and Susie Schmitt testified before the New Mexico House Judiciary Committee on House Bill 4, the New Mexico Civil Rights Act, as the parents of Carmela and Rex who were denied adequate health care at the Santa Fe Adult Detention Facility in November of 2019. Dozens of others testified before this hearing on the New Mexico Civil Rights Act that would permit "an individual to bring a claim against a public body or person acting on behalf of or under the authority of a public body for a violation of the individual's rights, privileges, or immunities," or essentially, revoke the defense of qualified immunity because the arduous process to prove that rights have been violated has abrogated these rights for too many years.

Qualified immunity is a judicially created defense for individual government employees that was established in the case of Pierson v. Ray by the US Supreme Court in 1967. It requires "a plaintiff to prove not only that his or her rights were violated but that the right at issue was so clearly established that any reasonably competent official would have known that." Rosenstock explained that the meaning of "clearly established" has become too difficult because the Supreme Court and federal appeals courts have interpreted it to mean that the plaintiff must show prior Supreme Court or Court of Appeals cases that should have put the official on notice that their conduct was unconstitutional or so similar to their case that they can't get past that defense. The absurdity of the defense is that it is highly unlikely, to say the least, that any governmental defendant has read any of the cases that are supposed to put them on "notice." The New Mexico Civil Rights Act ensures that people have a meaningful chance to have their day in state court. The Civil Rights Act also allows the court to award reasonable litigation expenses and attorneys' fees to any person who prevails in the civil rights action. The act does not, however, allow for punitive damages.

After the bill passed the State Government, Elections, and Indian Affairs Committee, a new iteration of the bill substituted language that changed several components:

- Claims brought pursuant to the New Mexico Civil Rights Act shall be brought exclusively against a public body, which would be held liable for individuals under the authority of that body. Many see this compromise as a failure to identify individuals who are guilty of civil rights violations and should be removed from the system.
- Damages would be capped at $2 million, including costs and attorney fees, to assuage concerns brought by state and local government entities that damages could bankrupt them. Interest rates and cost-of-living increases were factored in.

A slew of social justice and advocacy groups testified in favor of the bill, affirming that the act would finally make public agencies and those representing agencies accountable for violating people's civil rights. Groups included YUCCA (youth group organizing for climate justice), ACLU, Equality New Mexico (LGBTQ), AFSCME Union, NAACP, League of Women Voters, The Innocence Project, Bold Futures, Institute for Justice (a libertarian law firm), Americans for Prosperity, New Mexico Moms Demand Action (gun violence), Coalition of Sexual Assault Programs, National Police Accountability Project, Sierra Club Rio Grande Chapter, and APD Forward (advocates for reform within the Albuquerque Police Department). Former New Mexico Supreme Court Justice Richard Bossom, who served on the Civil Rights Committee that held public hearings to develop the bill, also testified in its favor.

Interestingly, representatives of several acequias, soil and water conservation districts, and land grants suggested that the bill should be amended to protect these kinds of small political subdivisions of the state from lawsuits that might cause them to lose their lands or impact their volunteers. House Speaker Brian Egolf responded to these concerns (he, Georgene Lewis, and Joseph Cervantes sponsored the bill) by claiming these are rather "far-fetched fears" and clarifying that under the law, land is not subject to seizure.

Most of the arguments raised by people representing law enforcement, and some cops themselves, insisted that the focus of this act is retribution against them (Judiciary Chair Gail Chasey rebuked one policeman for stating, "They want to get even with law enforcement") and that the focus should be on police training and reform, not punishment. Representatives of municipal and county governments, including Santa Fe County and Sandoval County, all argued that the act would open a floodgate of lawsuits and increase their insurance rates.

In his response to the public comment, Egolf stated that his overall impression of the testimony was that those who expressed their opposition failed to express any concern for the victims of abuse that so many of those advocating for the act raised in their testimony. In particular, the aunt of Omaree Varela, who was killed by his parents and failed in so many ways by the government agencies assigned to protect him, made a tearful plea for the passage of this act to bring those agencies to account. After a four-hour hearing the Judiciary Committee voted eight to four to pass. It was passed into law and became effective on July 1, 2021.

Ike Sues the County

On February 25, 2021, Ike, representing Carmela's estate, filed suit in Rio Arriba District Court against the Santa Fe County Board of Commissioners and its employees: Santa Fe Public Safety Director Pablo Sedillo; Santa Fe County Detention Center Warden Derek Williams; Medical Director Dr. Melquiades Olivares; and Correctional Officers Lieutenant Rojas and Captain Rios.

As mentioned previously, the Santa Fe County Adult Detention Facility has a long history of incompetence and neglect of its inmates.

As noted in the lawsuit, "in 2003 the United States Department of Justice found that the Center [Facility] provided inadequate medical care in the areas of intake, screening, referral, acute care, chronic care, and medical administration and management; that there was an improper delay in responding to inmate requests for medical treatment that put them at risk for worsening illness; and that often the treatment provided was substandard. The Justice Department findings concluded: 'As a result, inmates at the Detention Center with serious medical needs are at a risk for harm.'"

The Justice Department laid out requirements that the county needed to meet to avoid litigation, and in 2005 Annabelle Romero was hired as Corrections Director. Under her leadership the county brought the jail into compliance and then entered into a settlement agreement in 2008. Romero continued to implement reforms to bring the Facility into compliance with national standards.

In 2011 Santa Fe County officials hired Pablo Sedillo in the newly created position of County Public Safety Director. Defendant in Ike's lawsuit, Sedillo had previously been terminated from his job as a warden at an Arizona jail as a result of serious security problems at the facility, including a prison riot and allegations that a gang within the jail was smuggling drugs with the cooperation of the guards. According to the lawsuit, "Defendant Sedillo was well connected in the New Mexico Democratic Party." Shortly after Sedillo's hiring the county fired Romero with no reasons given for her termination.

Conditions in the jail began to deteriorate once again under Sedillo's watch. Ike's lawsuit cited cases of other inmates who died because of improper and inadequate medical care that resulted in the county paying hundreds of thousands of dollars to settle wrongful death lawsuits. Like Carmela's case, their deaths could be attributed to terrible conditions and/or illegal drug use in the jail. Correctional officers were charged with and implicated in the sale and/or use of unlawful drugs in the jail.

As opioid drug use escalated throughout the United States during these years, New Mexico especially suffered. According to a recent Legislative Finance Committee Report, between 1990 and 2018 the New Mexico death toll from substance abuse was over 38,000 and by 2018, death due to substance abuse accounted for 11 percent of all deaths. Health experts called for Santa Fe County to provide opiate based treatment to opiate dependent inmates at the Santa Fe County Adult Detention Facility because that is the most effective treatment available and does not require inmates to have to go through the painful, sometimes fatal, process of withdrawal.

In 2017 the Bernalillo County Detention Center began implementing Medication-Assisted Treatment (MAT) that provides guidelines for the use of buprenorphine (Suboxone) and methadone for the treatment of persons suffering from Opioid Use Disorder. According to the lawsuit, "despite being advised by experts that MAT was the standard of care for inmates suffering from Opioid Use Disorder, Defendants refused to adopt and implement such a program. Rather, Defendants offered only occasional treatment with Naltrexone [a second-line treatment far less effective than Suboxone or methadone]." The lawsuit documented the many experts and hearings that were held in Santa Fe County over deleterious conditions at the jail and the need for the County to implement the MAT program.

Attorneys Rosenstock and Daniel Yohalem of Santa Fe filed the lawsuit in Rio Arriba District Court against Defendant County of Santa Fe under the New Mexico Tort Claims Act and brought federal law claims against all the defendants pursuant to the Americans With Disabilities Act ("ADA") and Section 504 of the Rehabilitation Act of 1973 ("Section 504"). They requested a six-person jury trial and asked for compensatory damages; punitive damages against Defendants Sedillo, Williams, Olivares, Rojas, and Rios; pre- and post-judgment interest; and attorneys' fees and costs.

If the New Mexico Civil Rights Act, which was described previously, had been enacted before Carmela's death, a case such as this could have been heard in state court, rather than federal court. Ike was disappointed in the compromise that failed to identify individuals who were guilty of civil rights violations and who should have been removed from the system. Under federal law, those individuals who were negligent in Carmela's death could be held accountable through punitive damages, though it would be an uphill battle.

Meanwhile, Ike and Susie Schmitt continued gathering signatures on their grand jury petition, and on March 25 they submitted a petition of over 3,000 signatures to the Santa Fe County Manager calling for the First Judicial District Court to impanel a grand jury "to investigate acts of malfeasance, misfeasance, and any other illegal act committed by any individuals associated with or employed by the Santa Fe County Adult Detention Facility and the County of Santa Fe."

After submitting a copy of the petition to the county manager, Ike requested to speak during the public comment period at the Santa Fe County Commission meeting on March 30 to make sure the commissioners were aware of the petition. He was allotted three minutes. He told the commissioners that his daughter Carmela was twice a victim: first, of the doctors and big pharma that created the opioid epidemic in northern New Mexico that has taken so many lives and destroyed so many families; and second, of the abuse and negligence of the prison system. On November 8, the day before Carmela died at the hospital, one of the officers who had abused her at the Detention Facility was arrested at the jail for possession of methamphetamine. "There are as many drugs in the jail as there are in the street," Ike told the commissioners.

In April of 2021 Santa Fe County filed a motion to dismiss Ike's lawsuit, but Senior US District Judge Robert C. Brack then issued his decision on what charges could proceed to trial. Most of the charges leveled against the County would go forward: failure to implement a MAT (Medication Assisted Treatment) at the jail; failure to treat Carmela's OUD (Opioid Use Disorder) with Suboxone; allowing the jail to remain in an unsanitary condition; the policy of shackling; and an account of battery for administering Narcan against Carmela's will. (Narcan is administered for an overdose; Carmela did not overdose.) Except for Dr. Melquiades Olivares, whose failure to treat Carmela's OUD was allowed to proceed, the other named defendants were dismissed on the basis of qualified immunity. The case would be heard in Magistrate Court, and a December 2 status hearing was scheduled.

Rex Corcoran, Jr.'s estate filed a wrongful death lawsuit on November 5, 2021 against the Santa Fe County Board of County Commissioners and numerous employees of the Santa Fe County Adult Detention Facility claiming his death was due to their negligence and mistreatment. Rex had been receiving methadone from New Mexico Treatment Services and also suffered from Hepatitis C. Both these conditions were documented at his intake, but he was cleared for "General Population," not "Medical Housing." He suffered severe withdrawal and infections and died two weeks after being admitted to jail. The Magistrate Court of Santa Fe had remanded him to the Detention Facility for seven days for failure to pay certain fees.

The complaint documented the many stymied efforts of Rex's mother to get in touch with her son after he was taken into custody. When they spoke by phone on November 6, she assured him that she would be there to pick him up on November 12, the day he would be released from his seven-day court-mandated stay. He already sounded fearful and hung up abruptly. Despite repeated attempts to speak with her son or check on his well-being, she was never notified of his deteriorating condition and when finally able to talk on the phone with an officer, she was told he was "fine." The next—and last—time she saw him was in the hospital ICU on life support.

In a *New York Times* Opinion piece, the editors said this about the concept of parole: "Parole has a complicated history in this country, one that helps explain how we got into the crisis of mass incarceration and maybe how we might find a way out." They go on to say that when it began in the US in the 19th century it was envisioned as a rehabilitation tool but has now, through fear tactics, become one of the "pillars" of mass incarceration. In the case of Rex and Carmela, alleged parole violations became a death sentence.

Numerous parties employed at the Detention Facility were named in the Corcoran lawsuit (filed by the law firm of Rothstein Donatelli): the Warden, Derek Williams; seven officers ranking from lieutenant to corporal; the supervising doctor, Melquiades Olivares; and several nurses.

On November 6, family and friends gathered at the Santa Fe County Adult Detention Facility to mark the second anniversary of the deaths of Rex and Carmela. The groups also included family members of men who had died at the Rio Arriba Detention Center. Officially relegated to a dirt parking lot adjacent to the jail, participants decided to march down the road to the building with their signs and chants of "Say her name" and "Say his name!"

PHOTO BY BETH WALD

Demonstration at the Santa Fe County Adult Detention Facility

PHOTO BY BETH WALD

Susie and Ike

Settlement

Ike initially wanted the lawsuit to go to trial, to make those people identified in the suit accountable. When Santa Fe County offered a settlement agreement, he decided that he didn't want to put his grandson through any more trauma. He established a trust in the name of his grandson Andres and Andres's sister, Maria.

On September 27, Ike and Susie Schmitt protested in front of the John Gaw Meem Courthouse on Grant Street to proclaim that the settlements they received in their lawsuits against Santa Fe County weren't the justice they wanted. What they wanted was to protect the health, safety, and welfare of inmates at the Detention Facility, where the *Santa Fe New Mexican* reported three more deaths in just over a month. Under the portal at the historic county building Schmitt responded to the media's question as to why she kept protesting and petitioning the county for redress. "So my son's death wasn't in vain. I want change at the jail. It is acting as the judge, jury, and executioner. They murdered my son."[65]

Ramón Garcia

Ike and Susie in front of county building

Both Ike and Schmitt said they would rather see the money the county has paid out for settlements of deaths at the jail—$5,856,500 tax dollars that they know of—put to better use to improve conditions at the facility: better training and pay for the guards; implementing the MAT program (Medically Assisted Treatment) that provides addicts with the drugs they need so they don't have to go through withdrawal in jail; and making sure the medical staff is on duty 24/7. The medical director, an MD, is there only six hours a day.

In their press release Ike and Schmitt also called for the termination of those whose negligence they believe led to the deaths of their children: Santa Fe Public Safety Director Pablo Sedillo, Santa Fe Adult Detention Facility Warden Derek Williams, and Medical Director Melquiades Olivares. While the settlement money each estate received from the county would be put in trusts for Carmela and Rex's children, they remained angry that no one at the Detention Facility had been held accountable.

During the protest Santa Fe County Commissioners Rudy Garcia and Henry Roybal came outside for a break and were stopped by Schmitt, who asked them to sign the petition asking for a grand jury investigation into Carmela and Rex's deaths. The commissioners didn't sign the petition but Garcia told her that "I've been talking with the warden" and would "talk to Commissioner Roybal about it." Garcia's term would be over in December. Carmela and Rex died in 2019. The county commission had done nothing to address the conditions at the jail since then. Ike, Schmitt, and a family friend and former county manager (1979-1980), Ramón Garcia, each had three minutes during the public comment period at the commission meeting—after waiting four hours on the portal—to make their case for change at the jail. Will those changes ever be made?

The Final Chapter

In many of our conversations about his grandson Andres, Ike told me all he wanted was to stay alive until Andres turned 18 and could legally access his trust and be on his own. Ike and Andres were at my house helping pick cherries on July 2, 2024. I listened to the easy banter between the two of them and hoped that Ike's wish to see Andres turn 18 would come true.

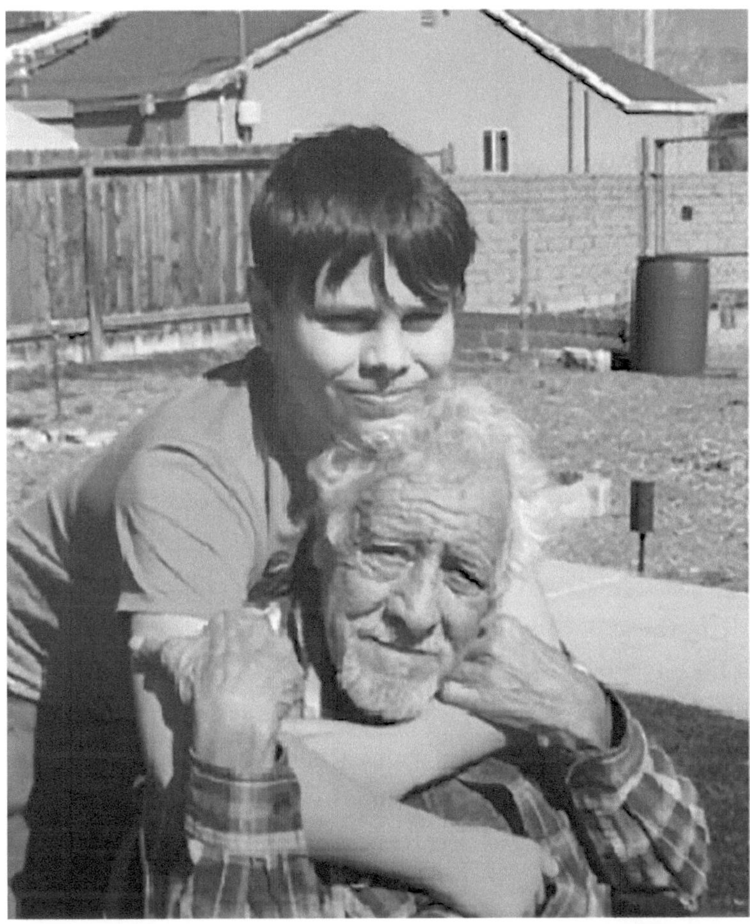

Andres and Ike

Ike didn't make it. He died on July 3 of a massive heart attack. He and Andres were in Llanito de La Madera, visiting his cousin, when the family found him outside, slumped over in a chair.

Elisa, Andres, and Ike

Andres went to live with his aunt Elisa, in Albuquerque. Elisa, a child psychologist, is a devoted aunt and was especially close to her dad. After Ike died, she had to step up and arrange the funeral, attend to his house and two German Shepard dogs in Servilleta Plaza, and do all the things one has to do when a family member dies. I don't know if Ike ever legally, or verbally, expressed what he wanted in terms of a funeral or memorial—he was a non-believer in a large Catholic family. But after a funeral mass filled with extended family and friends, Elisa arranged to have his ashes strewn atop his favorite peak in La Madera, along with a gathering of close friends and family

Ike on top of La Madera mountain

When I arrived in Servilleta Plaza for the gathering to spread his ashes, there was chaos. One of Ike's grandsons, who climbed with Elisa to the top of the mountain, disappeared on the way down with his very young son, and a search was called with the local volunteer fire departments responding. Ike's circle of friends who didn't volunteer to climb—most of us are in our seventies—hung around the house waiting for news. Finally, we gathered together and told our collective stories. Moises, who despite being ostracized by Ike in his later years, was part of the gathering and told the story of how Emilio's cops had planted drugs in his truck and busted him. Richard talked of his long friendship with Ike dating back to the Oficina de Leya days. I told the story of how Ike stepped into a potential brawl between a drunk and one of our friends acting like a rooster at the Chamisa Inn and stopped the fight.

PHOTO BY LUIS PEÑA

Servilleta gathering: Quentin Wilson, Deborah Begel, Kay Matthews, Andres Stone, Deborah Kearns, Richard Rosenstock, Wilfredo Vigil

The search party finally found the lost grandson and son around 5 o'clock, unharmed, after most of us were on our way home. Elisa and the family still at the house buried the rest of Ike's ashes beside his son Antonio's ashes in a fenced-in little yard near the house. Antonio died in the mid 1990s in an accidental shooting in Albuquerque. Along with Carmela's death, it was one of the most traumatic events in Ike's life, a life that what most people would consider nonending trauma: serving in special forces in Vietnam; beating up an off-duty cop and ending up in jail; fighting a political machine that ran people's lives for 20 years. But Ike was a warrior, in the best sense of the word: If there's something wrong then something needs to be done to make it right.

As I was finishing this book another warrior died. Barbara Lubin was a longtime activist based in the Bay Area and one of the founders of the Middle East Children's Alliance (MECA), an organization that supports Palestinian children in Gaza and the West Bank. In a statement released by MECA, Lubin had this to say about her activism:

"I think what carries me on is my anger at injustice. I know a lot of people say it's not good to be angry, but in reality, it's the anger at the unfairness in this world that just spurs me on. When I think something is really wrong, I'm not going to be quiet. I get up, and I fight, and I try and change it."

Ike at the Rio Grande

This was Ike's mantra as well. Despite all the obstacles, all the setbacks, all the difficulties (his computer and internet skills were negligible), and all that might be classified as failures, Ike always got up to try again. Whenever I would commiserate with him about the setbacks and failures, his response was always the same. "In the larger scheme of things, it may be that we lost, but in the smaller scheme of things, you never know who you may have impacted in a positive way or what you might have changed for the better." My life was certainly impacted in knowing Ike and I'm forever grateful for that.

Epilogue

Ike's recall petition against Rio Arriba County Commissioner Alex Naranjo lingered in the New Mexico Supreme Court (the petition was handed to Luis Peña) until July of 2025, a little over a week after the first anniversary of Ike's death, when the Court dismissed it. Reacting to the recall dismissal, Luis Peña told the *Santa Fe New Mexican* that "Legal outcomes do not erase moral responsibility."

To reiterate, Naranjo attempted to relocate the statue of conquistador Juan de Oñate at the Rio Arriba County Complex in Española in September of 2023, outside of a public meeting and in concert with other county officials. That relocation was postponed after days of demonstrations and vigils by Native Americans and Nuevomexicanos that resulted in the shooting attack of a protester by an alleged racist.

Naranjo's attorney appealed the state court decision, arguing that the recall shouldn't proceed because there was never an open meeting in which Naranjo violated the Open Meetings Act, in that the Act only applies to a quorum of commission board members, not an individual. At the Supreme Court hearing, one of the judges responded that all the emails submitted as evidence in district court indicate it was the commission, not just Naranjo, that decided to move the Oñate statue to the county complex. She was referring to emails sent by County Manager Jeremy Maestas and Sheriff Billy Merrifield in which Maestas claimed that the decision was made by the commission, not just Naranjo (the emails were revealed in a public request from Peña).

Contrary to the judge's assessment, the Supreme Court's dismissal claimed that district court did not decide that "the County Commission made the decision or that Commissioner Naranjo, along with a second commissioner (establishing a quorum), made the decision. Instead, the district court's inquiry was limited to whether

Commissioner Naranjo or County Manager Maestas made the decision. That legal conclusion was in error, as Commissioner Naranjo could not violate the OM [Open Meetings Act] as a single member of the County Commission acting alone."

Richard Rosenstock, attorney for Ike and Peña, said that this was a "poorly reasoned and written opinion." What the court should have done was remand the case back to the district court, which would have determined there was a quorum and that Naranjo was part of that quorum, based on the emails. "I was expecting this decision from day one. Tell me one case in the last 50 years involving land grant rights and water rights and any Democratic official where it's turned out favorably."

There is an opportunity for justice, however, in the recall attempt. On May 13th, 2025, Native Americans Jacob Johns and Malaya Corrine Peixinho filed tort claims lawsuits against Rio Arriba County officials who they claim "ignored the threat of violence and failed to protect peaceful demonstrators from a politically motivated, near-fatal shooting by an armed assailant on September 28, 2023." This is the day that MAGA supporter Ryan Martinez shot Johns in the stomach, causing severe injury, at the demonstration in front of the Rio Arriba County Complex where people had gathered to protest the reinstallation of the statue (it originally stood at the Oñate Monument and Visitor's Center in Alcalde). Martinez (who was convicted of aggravated battery and aggravated assault) also pointed his gun at Peixinho.

The lawsuit, filed by civil rights attorney Mariel Nanasi—who is also the director of the New Energy Economy—names the county officials who were negligent in providing law enforcement to an event they knew might erupt in violence because of the heightened feelings that surround the controversial conquistador Oñate: Rio Arriba County Sheriff Billy Merrifield, Undersheriff John Doe, County Commissioners Alex M. Naranjo, Brandon M. Bustos, Moises A. Morales Jr., and County Manager Jeremy Maestas.

According to the lawsuit, Sheriff Merrifield (who recently died unexpectedly) had "warned the County Commission days in advance of the high probability of unrest, citing intelligence that the situation could lead to 'riot,' 'physical force,' and even 'deadly force.' Incredibly, rather than increase police presence, County deputies left the site entirely." As documented earlier, at the District Court hearing that granted the petition to recall Naranjo, emails between Ryan Martinez and Jeremey Maestas were provided, revealing Martinez's lobbying to reinstate the statue.

The plaintiffs claim the county's actions, or inactions, "violated the New Mexico Civil Rights Act and Tort Claims Act. The suits seek damages for emotional distress, physical injuries, and long-term disability."

Terms — People — Places

1848 Treaty of Guadalupe Hidalgo — ending US/Mexican War

1972 US Forest Service Region Three Policy Plan (the 1968 Hassell Report)

1984 Democratic Convention in San Francisco for Jesse Jackson

Activists Moises Morales — Pedro Archuleta — Andres Valdez — Susana Valdez — Barbara Manzanares — Santiago Juarez

Agua/Caballos timber sale — located in the Vallecitos Federal Sustained Yield Unit

Agua/Caballos lawsuit — filed against the Forest Service by environmentalists

Agua/Caballos Draft Environmental Impact Statement (DEIS) — released by the Forest Service as required by the National Environmental Policy Act (NEPA)

Alamo-Diner Sale — timber sale on the Camino Real Ranger District

Alan Siegal — arrested by Emilio Naranjo on a misdemeanor charge and illegally delivered to a federal prison in Texas

Alex Atencio — Rio Arriba County Republican Chair

Alex Naranjo — nephew of Emilio Naranjo; Rio Arriba County Commissioner; brother of Nick Naranjo

Alfonso Chacon — logger in the Vallecitos Federal Sustained Yield Unit

Alianza Federal de las Mercedes — Reies Lopez Tijerina's land grant organization

Americans for Prosperity — grassroots organization in Albuquerque

Andy Caffrey — Earth First! Media Center

Annabelle Romero — Santa Fe County Corrections Director (fired without cause)

Andres Valdez — norteño activist accused by Emilio Naranjo of bombing a bar

Antonio "Ike" DeVargas — founding member of Rio Arriba County La Raza Unida Party; founding member of La Companía de Ocho; Chicano activist

Antonio Griego — Rio Arriba County Sheriff's Deputy

APD Forward — advocates for reform within the Albuquerque Police Department

Armendariz et al.-v.-Santa Fe County — class action lawsuit against Santa Fe County

Arthur Rodarte — defeated Emilio Naranjo in state senate race

Barbara Romo — 13th Judicial District Attorney

Benjamin Chavez — Second Judicial District Judge

Bill Redmond — Third Congressional District Representative

Bill Richardson — Third Congressional District Representative

Billy Merrifield — Rio Arriba County Sheriff

Bob Rothstein — civil rights attorney

Bold Futures — advocacy for women and people of color

Bolo One and Bolo Two sales — first timber sales bought by La Companía de Ocho

Borracho timber sale — located in the Carson National Forest

Brandon M. Bustos — Rio Arriba County Commissioner

Brian Egolf — Speaker of the New Mexico House of Representatives

Brown Berets Crusade for Justice — Chicano activist organization

Bruce Duran — Jemez Mountains Electric Co-op board member

Bruce Hamilton — officer in the Sierra Club

Bryan Bird — Conservation Biologist/Appeals Coordinator of Forest Guardians; Secretary of the Rio Grande Chapter of the Sierra Club

Camino Real Ranger District — Carson National Forest

Carl Anthony — African-American director of Urban Habitat; board of directors president at Earth Island Institute

Carmela DeVargas — Ike's daughter who died in 2019

Carol Miller — health activist from Ojo Sarco; succeeded Ike as director of La Clinica del Pueblo de Rio Arriba; nominated by Greens to run in Third Congressional District

Carson National Forest Plan — promulgated in 1985

Carson Forest Watch — environmental organization based in the Camino Real Ranger District

Charlotte Talberth — former Forest Guardians board member; wife of John Talberth

Chellis Glendinning — writer and activist from Chimayó

Chicanos Associated Student Organization — founder of New Mexico La Raza Unida Party

Chris Wilson — author of *Myth of Santa Fe: Creating a Modern Regional Tradition*

Christine Bustos — Rio Arriba County Commissioner

Cliff Larsen — Santa Fe Group of the Sierra Club Conservation Chair

Collaborative Forest Restoration Program (CFRP)—initiated by Senator Jeff Bingaman

Courtney White — chair of the Santa Group of the Sierra Club Conservation Committee; co-founder of the Quivira Coalition

Cynthia McKinney — US Representative and sponsor of the National Forest Protection and Restoration Act

Daniel Yohalem — Santa Fe attorney who represented Ike

Danny Garcia — Rio Arriba County Commissioner

Danny Lyon — filmmaker and photographer

Danny Lyon film “Little Boy” 1977

Darnell — timber operator in the Carson National Forest

Dave Foreman — founder of Earth First!

David Benavides — water rights and land grant attorney at Northern New Mexico Legal Aid

David Correia — author of *Properties of Violence: Law and Land Grant Struggle in Northern New Mexico;* professor at UNM

David Koch — oil and corporate magnate largely responsible for climate disruption

David Orr — chair of the national Sierra Club No Logging Task Force

Democrats for Progress — founded after La Raza Unida Party dissolved

Dennis Valdez — founding member of La Companía de Ocho

Derek Williams — Warden at the Santa Fe County Detention Facility

Diana Trujillo — El Rito District Ranger who succeeded Kurt Winchester

Don Diego de Vargas — statue in Cathedral Park in Santa Fe

Donald Orie — initiated grand jury indictment of Rio Arriba County with Ike

Donna House — Native American activist

Douglas Wood — First Judicial Assistant District Attorney

Draft Environmental Impact Statements — required by National Environmental Policy Act (NEPA)

Duke City Lumber Company — subsidiary of the transnational Hansen Industries (then Idaho Timber Corporation); operator in the Vallecitos Federal Sustained Yield Unit

Earth Island Institute — non-profit environmental organization

Edwin Mechem — US District Judge

El Grupo — coalition of norteño activists

Elisa DeVargas — Ike's daughter and guardian of Ike's grandson Andres

El norte — northern New Mexico

Emilio Naranjo — Rio Arriba County sheriff; chair of Rio Arriba County Democratic Party; US Marshal; state senator; corrupt county patron

Emily Miggins — Rethink Paper, a project of Earth Island Institute

Endangered Species Act — US law protecting flora and fauna from extinction

Eric Serna — ran to replace US Representative Bill Richardson

Española Fiesta Council — group that supports the statue of Conquistador Juan de Oñate

Federal Sustained Yield Act (federally mandated) — designated in the 1940s to directly benefit impoverished rural communities

Felipe Martinez — founding member of Las Comunidades

Felipito Diversity Unit — site of first timber sale awarded to La Companía as subcontractor of Duke City

Final Environmental Impact Statements — required by National Environmental Policy Act (NEPA)

Forest Conservation Council — Santa Fe environmental group

Forest Guardians — Santa Fe environmental group

Forest Trust — non-profit forestry consultant based in Santa Fe

Gabe Aldaz and Lucas Culin — Vallecitos teenagers

Gail Chasey — Judiciary Chair of New Mexico State Senate

Ganados del Valle — northern New Mexico agricultural cooperative

George Grossman — member of the Rio Grande Chapter of the Sierra Club; Santa Fe Group's Forest Issues Chair; Carson Forest Issues Chair; National Sierra Club Environmental Hero in 1992

Gino Romero — North Central Solid Waste Authority manager

Graciela Terrazas — El Rito District Ranger

Green Party of New Mexico

Greg Bemis — Republican who ran for US Representative against Democrat Bill Richardson

Grove Burnett — environmental lawyer

Hassell Report — 1968 management policy — or "The People of Northern New Mexico and the National Forests"

Henry Carey — director of Forest Trust

Henry Roybal — Santa Fe County Commissioner

Institute for Justice — a libertarian law firm

Jackson Lumber Company — Carson National Forest designated operator

Jacob Johns — Native activist shot in the stomach by MAGA member Ryan Martinez

Jacques Tank timber sale — located in Carson National Forest

Jake Kosek — author of *Understories: The Political Life of Northern New Mexico Forests*; professor at UC Berkeley

James Martinez — Rio Arriba County Commission Chairman

Jan-Willem Jansens — member of Forest Trust

Janice Varela — member of La Gente del Rio Pecos

Jason Linyard — First Judicial District Court judge

Jeremy Maestas — Rio Arriba County Manager

Jesse Jackson—ran for president in 1984 under the Rainbow Coalition

JMEC Trustees 4 Change — watchdog group of Jemez Mountain Electric Coop

Joanie Berde — founder of Carson Forest Watch

John Bedell — Carson Forest Supervisor

John Horning — member of Forest Guardians

John Muir Project — a project of Earth Island Institute

John N. Nieto-Phillips — author of *The Language of Blood: The Making of Spanish-American Identity in New Mexico 1880s-1930s*

John Talberth — co-founder of Forest Conservation Council and member of Forest Guardians

Joseph Lewandowski — manager of North Central Solid Waste Authority

Joseph Sanchez — State Representative District 40

Juan de Oñate — Spanish Conquistador

Juan Jose Peña — La Raza Unida Party member

Kieran Suckling — board member and director of the Arizona-based Center for Biological Diversity

Kurly Tlapoyawa — archaeologist, author, and ethnohistorian

Kurt Winchester — El Rito District Ranger; assistant Carson National Forest Supervisor

La Clinica del Pueblo del Rio Arriba — a free or low-cost medical clinic (Ike was the director from 1980 to 1982)

La Compania de Ocho — logging company founded by Ike, Mike Peña, Patricio Valdez, Manuel Gurule, Steve Chavez, and Dennis Valdez

La Cooparación del Pueblo (The Unified People) — economic projects organization in Tierra Amarilla

La Cooperative Agricola (the Agricultural Cooperative) — farming projects organization in Tierra Amarilla

La Herencia del Norteños Unidos — coalition of groups that included La Madera Forest Products, the rural electric co-op, cattlemen's associations, La Companía de Ocho, and Las Comunidades

La Jicarita News — a journal of environmental politics (Kay Matthews and Mark Schiller, editors)

la lucha — Spanish for the fight

La Manga Jo timber sale — La Companía de Ocho sale in the Vallecitos Federal Sustained Yield Unit

La Manga lawsuit — filed against the Forest Service by environmentalists

La Raza Unida Party — Chicano activist group originally organized in Texas but with large membership in New Mexico; New Mexico chapter of La Raza Unida founded by the Chicanos Associated Student Organization at Highland University in Las Vegas in 1971

La Sierra — activist group from San Luis, Colorado

Larry Henson — US Forest Service Regional Forester

Larry Miller — activist from Ojo Sarco

Las Comunidades — designated operation in the Vallecitos Federal Sustained Yield Unit

Legislative Finance Committee Report — on New Mexico substance abuse deaths

Leo Jaramillo — Rio Arriba County Commissioner; New Mexico State Senator

Leonard Lindquist — Carson Forest Supervisor

Leonard Lucero — Carson Forest Supervisor

Linda Pedro — Chimayo activist; supported Jesse Jackson's Rainbow Coalition; helped create Americans with Disability Act of 1990

Lisa Krooth — director of Northern New Mexico Legal Aid

Lori Osterstock — Española District Ranger

Lucas Córdova — Jemez Mountains Electric Co-op board member

Lucas Culin and Gabe Aldaz — Vallecitos teenagers

Lucia Sanchez — Rio Arriba County Manager

Lucy Lippard — author and activist

Luis Peña — norteño activist; petitioner in Alex Naranjo recall

Luis Torres — director of La Madera Forest Products

Madera Forest Products Association — started 1988 and included membership of all the largely Hispano communities adjacent to the Vallecitos Federal Sustained Yield Unit

Malaya Corrine Peixinho — Native American who filed tort claims lawsuits against Rio Arriba County officials after shooting at the County Complex

Manny Aragon — New Mexico State Senator whose name was removed from a government building after he was convicted and sent to prison for conspiracy to defraud the state

Manuel Archuleta — La Raza Unida Party member in San Miguel County

Manuel Gurule — founding member of La Companía de Ocho

Maria Varela — norteño activist; founder of Los Ganados del Valle

Marie Ward — First District Court judge

Mariel Nanasi — civil rights attorney; director of the New Energy Economy

Mary Carmack-Altwies — First Judicial District Attorney

Max Córdova — president of the Truchas land grant; founder of La Montana de Truchas

Medication-Assisted Treatment (MAT) — substance abuse treatment used in jails

Dr. Melquiades Olivares — Medical Director at the Santa Fe County Adult Detention Facility

Mexican spotted owl — endangered species

Mexican spotted owl lawsuit — filed against the Forest Service by environmental groups

Michael Naranjo — Emilio Naranjo's nephew

Mike Cherin — Forest Guardians' chief canvasser

Mike Espy — US Secretary of Agriculture

Mike Peña — founding member of La Companía de Ocho

MM (The Minute Men) — implicated in Forest Guardians bomb threat

Moises Morales — La Raza Unida Party member; Rio Arriba County Commissioner

Nathana Bird — member of Ohkay Owingeh Pueblo; Associate Director of Tewa Women United

National Conservation Governance Committee — Sierra Club

National Environmental Policy Act (NEPA) — federal law requiring environmental analysis of proposed actions

National Forest Management Act (NFMA)—1976 federal law to protect forest ecosystems

National Forest Protection and Restoration Act — imposing limits on logging introduced by Rep. Cynthia McKinney

National Heritage Restoration Corps — part of National Forest Protection and Restoration Act

New Mexico Civil Rights Act — passed in 2021

New Mexico Tort Claims Act — Ike's lawsuit over daughter Carmela's death

Nick Naranjo — chairman of the Jemez Mountains Electric Co-op board; brother of Alex Naranjo; nephew of Emilio Naranjo

Norteño — relating to northern New Mexico

North Central Solid Waste Authority — Rio Arriba County private waste management company

Northern New Mexico Legal Services (or Legal Aid) — represented Madera Forest Products

Notice of Tort Claim — Ike's lawsuit over daughter Carmela's death

Oficina de Leya — law office in Tierra Amarilla

Omaree Varela — killed by his parents

Oñate Monument and Visitor's Center in Alcalde — original site of Juan de Oñate statue

Open Meetings Act (OMA) — "sunshine law" requiring governmental bodies to conduct official business in public

Pablo Sedillo — Santa Fe Public Safety Director; Defendant in Ike's lawsuit

Pat D'Andrea — member of El Grupo

Patricio Valdez — founding member of La Companía de Ocho

Patrick Herrera — ran/lost to be Jemez Mountains Electric Co-op board member

Paul Becker — Vallecitos Stables; Agua/Caballos lawsuit plaintiff

Pedro Archuleta — norteño activist targeted by FBI

Peter Romero — North Central Solid Waste Authority placed a lien on his property

Praxedis Ortega — representative of La Sierra

Protect Our Public Lands — project of Earth Island Institute

Purdue Pharma Sackler family — under indictment for false advertising of opioids

Ramón Garcia — former Santa Fe County manager (1979-1980)

Ramsey Logging Company — subcontractor in the Carson National Forest

Randy Schofield — rancher from Tres Piedras

Red Nation — coalition of Native activists in Albuquerque

Reies Lopez Tijerina — founder of Alianza Federales de Las Mercedes

Rethink Paper — project of Earth Island Institute

Rex Corcoran, Jr. — died at the Santa Fe County Adult Detention Facility

Richard Bossom — former New Mexico Supreme Court Justice

Richard Rosenstock — civil rights attorney; lawyer at La Oficina de Ley in Tierra Amarilla; represented La Companía de Ocho

Rio Arriba County Annex — renamed the Emilio Naranjo Building

Rio Grande Chapter of the Sierra Club — environmental organization representing all of New Mexico and part of Texas

Rio Grande Sierran — Sierra Club publication

Rio Grande Sun — Española weekly newspaper

Rio Pueblo/Rio Embudo Watershed Protection Coalition — watchdog group based in Peñasco area

Rios, Captain — correctional officer at the Santa Fe County Adult Detention Facility

Robert C. Brack — Senior US District Judge

Rodolfo Acuña — author of *Occupied America: A History of Chicanos*

Rojas, Lieutenant — correctional officer at the Santa Fe County Adult Detention Facility

Ron Lovato — governor of Ohkay Owingeh

Rudy Garcia — Santa Fe County Commissioner

Ryan Martinez — MAGA member who shot Native activist Jacob Johns

Sam Hitt — founder of Forest Guardians; worked at La Clinica in Tierra Amarilla; founder of Wild Watershed

San Miguel County Sheriff's Posse — a paramilitary-like group

Santa Fe Group of the Sierra Club (later called the Northern Group) — refused to support Zero Cut initiative

Saul Alinsky — community organizer

Sea Shepherds — environmental organization

Section 504 of the Rehabilitation Act of 1973 ("Section 504") — used in Ike's lawsuit over the death of daughter Carmela

Servilleta Plaza — norteño community; home of Ike

Southwest Center for Biological Diversity — environmental organization

Southwest Organizing Project (SWOP) — Chicano organization based in Albuquerque

Stan Crawford — Dixon author; board member of Jemez Mountains Electric Co-op board for District 5

Statue of Spanish Conquistador Juan de Oñate — removed from the Oñate Monument and Visitor's Center

Stet Edmonds — US Forest Service Taos District Timber Specialist

Steve Chavez — founding member of La Companía de Ocho

Steve Farber — attorney representing Ike

Stone Forest Industries — logging company in Colorado

Susie Schmitt — mother of Rex Corcoran; filed lawsuit over Rex's death

Taos Citizens Together — environmental group

The Innocence Project — non-profit legal advocacy organization

The National Forest Protection Alliance — advocated for end to commercial logging on public lands

Thor — Ike's black mastiff

Tom Udall — New Mexico US Representative; New Mexico US Senator

Tomás Compos — Rio Arriba County Manager

Toney Anaya — New Mexico Attorney General

Tony Povilitis — member of Greater San Juan Coalition

Tri-State — energy provider

Trial by Email — Sierra Club controversy over George Grossman

Truchas Land Grant (Nuestra Señora del Rosario San Fernando y Santiago Land Grant)

US Senator Joseph Montoya — Emilio Naranjo's mentor and supporter

United States Surveyor General — adjudicator of land grants

Urban Habitat — San Francisco advocacy group

Valle Grande timber sale — Carson National Forest

Vallecitos — norteño community

Vallecitos Association — advocacy group for labor timber practices

Vallecitos Lumber Mill — owned by Duke City

Vandana Shiva — Indian activist

Walter Kegel — Emilio Naranjo's attorney

Wildland Urban Interface (WUI) — critical wildfire area

Wilfred Romero — ran for Rio Arriba County Sheriff; associate warden at Penitentiary of New Mexico

Wilfredo Vigil — norteño activist; close friend of Ike

William (Bill) deBuys — author and conservationist

William D. Hurst — US Forest Service Region Three Forester

Wise Use — a movement founded by groups that support privatization and less government regulation under the guise of "stewardship"

YUCCA — youth group organizing for climate justice

Zero Cows Campaign — no cows on public lands

Zero Cut Campaign (later the National Forest Protection Campaign) — no commercial logging on public lands

Zia Company — a subcontractor of Los Alamos National Laboratory

End Notes

1. Interview with Ike, Raza Unida Oral History Project, Peter Malmgren, December 3, 2004.
2. Interview with Ike, La Jicarita and UNM Professor David Correia on July 15, 2008.
3. Interview with Ike, Raza Unida Oral History Project, Peter Malmgren, December 3, 2004.
4. Ibid.
5. Interview with Ike, La Jicarita and UNM Professor David Correia on July 15, 2008.
6. Interview with Ike, Raza Unida Oral History Project, Peter Malmgren, December 8, 2004.
7. Correia, David, *Properties of Violence: Law and Land Grant Struggle in Northern New Mexico*, Athens, Georgia, University of Kentucky Press, 2013.
8. Interview with Ike, La Jicarita and UNM Professer David Correia on July 15, 2008.
9. Ibid.
10. Ibid.
11. Ibid.
12. Ibid.
13. Rio Grande Sun, March 11, 1976.
14. Rosenstock, Richard, "The Decline of Patronismo in Rio Arriba County, 1975-77."
15. Ibid.
16. Interview with Ike, Raza Unida Oral History Project, Peter Malmgren, December 8, 2004.
17. Interview with Ike, La Jicarita and UNM Professor David Correia on July 15, 2008.
18. Santa Fe New Mexican, June 27, 1977.
19. Interview with Ike, La Jicarita and UNM Professor David Correia on July 15, 2008.
20. Kay Matthews, "Emilio Naranjo rises from the ashes to haunt us again," La Jicarita, July 19, 2019.

21. Interview with Ike, Raza Unida Oral History Project, Peter Malmgren, December 8, 2004.
22. Interview with Antonio "Ike" DeVargas, Ten Years Later," La Jicarita, December, 2005.
23. David Correia, "Vallecitos Federal Sustained Unit: From Agropastoralism to Sustained Yield Forestry," La Jicarita, May 2005, excerpted and edited from several of Correia's articles.
24. Ibid.
25. Matthews, Kay, *Culture Clash, Environmental Politics in New Mexico Forest Communities*, Santa Fe, Sunstone Press, 2015.
26. "Interview with Antonio "Ike" DeVargas, Ten Years Later," La Jicarita, December, 2005.
27. Ibid.
28. "Interview with Antonio DeVargas," La Jicarita, January, 1996.
29. Ibid.
30. Kay Matthews, "What's Happening in the Rest of New Mexico," La Jicarita, April, 1996.
31. Matthews, Kay, *Culture Clash, Environmental Politics in New Mexico Forest Communities*, Santa Fe, Sunstone Press, 2015.
32. Kay Matthews, "What's Happening in the Rest of New Mexico: A Meeting of Minds at the Oñate Center," La Jicarita, September, 1996.
33. Kay Matthews, "What's Happening in the Rest of New Mexico: Norteños Force Forest Service to Issue More Wood Permits," La Jicarita, October, 1996.
34. Kay Matthews, "What's Happening in the Rest of New Mexico: Roundtable Discussion Hopes to Tear Down Fences Between Norteños, Environmentalists, and Forest Service," La Jicarita, January, 1997.
35. Kay Matthews, "La Manga Timber Sale Controversy Rages On," La Jicarita, June/July, 1997.
36. "Interview with Antonio "Ike" DeVargas, Ten Years Later," La Jicarita, December, 2005.
37. Interview with Ike, Raza Unida Oral History Project, Peter Malmgren, December 3, 2004.
38. Matthews, Kay, *Culture Clash, Environmental Politics in New Mexico Forest Communities*, Santa Fe, Sunstone Press, 2015.

39. Ibid.
40. Ibid.
41. Courtney White, "Sierra Club Refuses to Participate in Bingaman's Roundtable," La Jicarita, August,1998.
42. Matthews, Kay, *Culture Clash, Environmental Politics in New Mexico Forest Communities*, Santa Fe, Sunstone Press, 2015.
43. Kosek, Jake, *Overstories: The Life of Northern New Mexico Forests*, Durham and London, Duke University Press, 2006.
44. Matthews, Kay, *Culture Clash, Environmental Politics in New Mexico Forest Communities*, Santa Fe, Sunstone Press, 2015.
45. Ibid.
46. Antonio "Ike" DeVargas, "Puntos de Vista," La Jicarita, October, 1997.
47. Kay Matthews, "Aguas/Caballos Proposed Projects Record of Decision Appealed," La Jicarita," September/October, 2002.
48. Ibid.
49. Kay Matthews," Agua/Caballos Again Appealed," La Jicarita, August/September, 2004.
50. Ibid.
51. Kay Matthews, "Environmentalists File Lawsuit to Stop Agua/ Caballos Timber Sale," La Jicarita, May, 2005.
52. Robert Trapp, "Trash Authority Customers Deserve Solid GM," Rio Grande Sun, January 4, 2018.
53. Kay Matthews, "North Central Solid Waste Authority: A Bureaucratic Nightmare," La Jicarita, September 6, 2021.
54. Kay Matthews, "Patronage: Alive and Well in Rio Arriba County," La Jicarita, August 29, 2019.
55. Kay Matthews, "Rio Arriba County Acknowledges its Solid Waste Ordinance is Arbitrary and Capricious," January 26, 2022.
56. Kurly Tlapoyawa, https://unseennewmexico.wordpress.com.
57. Kay Matthews, "Oñate, deVargas, General Lee, Andrew Jackson: White Nationalists Coming Down," La Jicarita, June 28, 2020.
58. Ibid.
59. Nieto-Phillips, John N., *The Language of Blood: The Making of Spanish-American Identity in New Mexico 1880s-1930s*, Albuquerque, University of New Mexico Press, 2008.

60. Wilson, Chris, *Myth of Santa Fe: Creating a Modern Regional Tradition*, Albuquerque, University of New Mexico Press, 1997.
61. Kay Matthews, "First Judicial Attorney General's Office Fails the People Once Again," La Jicarita, December 22, 2023.
62. Kay Matthews, "At the Rio Arriba Recall Hearing: A Cringe Worthy Event," La Jicarita, March 21, 2024.
63. Kay Matthews, "Recall Petition of Rio Arriba County Commissioner Alex Naranjo Can Proceed," La Jicarita, May 3, 2024.
64. Kay Matthews, "Sign the Petition for Carmela and Rex and Criminal Justice Reform," La Jicarita, February 9, 2020.
65. Kay Matthews, "Santa Fe County Pays Millions of Taxpayer Dollars for Wrongful Death Settlements," La Jicarita, September 28, 2022.

Acknowledgments

Many thanks go to Richard Rosenstock, Luis Peña, Peter Malmgren, Eric Shultz, David Correia, and Elisa DeVargas, who all contributed to this book, both in their involvement in Ike's politics and their collegial help with the manuscript and photos. Thanks also to Nighthawk Press publisher Rebecca Lenzini, editor Adrienne Pond, and Kelly Pasholk of Wink Visual Arts, whose design of the book makes it a pleasure to hold and read.

About the Author

Kay Matthews is the publisher of *La Jicarita*, an online journal of environmental politics that's been reporting in el norte since 1996. She's also the author of a number of books: two children's books; a series of hiking, backpacking, and cross-country skiing guides to northern New Mexico; *Culture Clash: Environmental Politics in New Mexico Forest Communities*; *Stories From Life's Other Side*; *Unf*#!ing Believable* (essays); and *¡No Se Vende! Water as a Right of the Commons*. She lives on a small farm in El Valle.

www.ingramcontent.com/pod-product-compliance
Ingram Content Group UK Ltd.
Pitfield, Milton Keynes, MK11 3LW, UK
UKHW041637190726
13854UKWH00006B/2551